Dr. Jekyll *and* Mr. Hyde

A Kaplan SAT Score-Raising Classic

Look for more Kaplan SAT Novels:

The Ring of McAllister: A Score-Raising Mystery
Featuring 1,046 Must-Know SAT Vocabulary Words

Frankenstein:
A Kaplan SAT Score-Raising Classic

Wuthering Heights:
A Kaplan SAT Score-Raising Classic

The Tales of Edgar Allan Poe:
A Kaplan SAT Score-Raising Classic

Coming in August 2005

The Scarlet Letter:
A Kaplan SAT Score-Raising Classic

Dr. Jekyll *and* Mr. Hyde

A Kaplan SAT Score-Raising Classic

by Robert Louis Stevenson

Simon & Schuster

New York ✦ London ✦ Sydney ✦ Toronto

Kaplan Publishing
Published by Simon & Schuster, Inc.
1230 Avenue of the Americas
New York, NY 10020

For bulk sales to schools, colleges, and universities, please contact: Order Department, Simon & Schuster, Inc. 100 Front Street, Riverside, NJ 08075. Phone: 1-800-223-2336. Fax: 1-800-943-9831.

For information regarding special discounts for other bulk purchases, please contact Simon & Schuster Special Sales at 1-800-456-6798 or business@simonandschuster.com

Kaplan® is a registered trademark of Kaplan, Inc.

Cover Design: Cheung Tai / Mark Weaver
Cover Illustration: Greg Copeland
Interior Page Design and Production: Lori Ulrich
Editor: Helena Santini

Manufactured in the United States of America

May 2005

10 9 8 7 6 5 4

Library of Congress Cataloging-in-Publication Data is available.

ISBN: 0-7432-6470-3

How To Use This Book

$\longrightarrow\!\!\!\blacktriangleright$

Dr. Jekyll and Mr. Hyde is not only filled with mystery and intrigue—it's also filled with SAT words! Now Kaplan makes it as easy as 1-2-3 for you to learn these vocabulary words as you read the stories.

On the right-hand pages you'll find the story of *Dr. Jekyll and Mr. Hyde* with words **bolded** throughout. These bolded words are frequently found on the SAT. On the left-hand pages, Kaplan defines these SAT words, as well as gives you the part of speech, pronunciation, and synonyms for each word—everything you need to know to improve your vocabulary and to ace the SAT.

Some of the most challenging vocabulary words found in *Dr. Jekyll and Mr. Hyde* aren't likely to appear on the SAT, but we thought you might want to learn those, too. That's why we've underlined them throughout the text and added their definitions to a glossary at the end of the book. After all—you never know where they might pop up next!

So what are you waiting for? Start reading!

TABLE OF CONTENTS

COUNTENANCE (<u>kown</u> tuh nuhns) *n.*
appearance, facial expression
Synonyms: face, features, visage

DISCOURSE (<u>dihs</u> kohrs) *n.*
conversation, expression of thought, the verbal
interchange of ideas
Synonyms: speaking, oration, dialogue, discussion

SENTIMENT (<u>sehn</u> tuh muhnt) *n.*
an attitude, thought, or judgment prompted by
feeling, a romantic or nostalgic feeling
Synonyms: idea, emotion

EMINENTLY (<u>ehm</u> uh nuhnt lee) *adv.*
prominently, obviously; in an outstanding manner
Synonyms: evidently; importantly, illustriously

AUSTERE (aw <u>steer</u>) *adj.*
stern, strict, unadorned
Synonyms: dour, bare, ascetic

MORTIFY (<u>mohr</u> tih fie) *v.* **-ing,-ied.**
1. to practice self-discipline by denying one's own
needs or desires
Synonyms: dismiss, shun, disregard
2. to humiliate or make someone feel shame
Synonyms: embarrass, humble, abase

INCLINE (ihn <u>klien</u>) *v.* **-ing,-ed.**
1. to have a specific tendency, to be predisposed
Synonyms: lean to, influence, impel, prefer
2. to bend or tilt upward
Synonyms: slope, slant, lean, deviate, point

REPROVE (rih <u>proov</u>) *v.* **-ing,-ed.**
to criticize or correct
Synonyms: rebuke, admonish, reprimand, chide,
reproach

DEMEANOUR or DEMEANOR (dih <u>meen</u> uhr) *n.*
one's behavior or conduct
Synonyms: attitude, disposition, manner, presence

CATHOLICITY (kaath uh <u>lihs</u> ih tee) *n.*
universality, comprehensive broadness
Synonyms: extent, generality, inclusiveness

STORY OF THE DOOR

Mr. Utterson the lawyer was a man of a rugged **countenance** who was never lighted by a smile; cold, scanty, and embarrassed in **discourse**; backward in **sentiment**; lean, long, dusty, dreary, and yet somehow lovable. At friendly meetings, and when the wine was to his taste, something **eminently** human beaconed from his eye. It was something indeed which never found its way into his talk, but which spoke not only in these silent symbols of the after-dinner face, but more often and loudly in the acts of his life. He was **austere** with himself, drank gin when he was alone to **mortify** a taste for vintages, and though he enjoyed the theatre, had not crossed the doors of one for twenty years. But he had an approved tolerance for others, sometimes wondering, almost with envy, at the high pressure of spirits involved in their misdeeds. In any extremity, he was **inclined** to help rather than to **reprove**. "I **incline** to Cain's heresy," he used to say quaintly. "I let my brother go to the devil in his own way." In this character it was frequently his fortune to be the last reputable acquaintance and the last good influence in the lives of downgoing men. And to such as these, so long as they came about his chambers, he never marked a shade of change in his **demeanour**.

No doubt the feat was easy to Mr. Utterson, for he was undemonstrative at the best, and even his friendships seemed to be founded in a similar **catholicity** of good-nature. It is the mark of a modest man to accept his friendly circle ready-made from the hands of opportunity, and that was the lawyer's way. His friends were

SINGULARLY (<u>sihn</u> gyuh luhr lee) *adv.*
uncommonly, peculiarly
Synonyms: unusually, oddly, rarely, uniquely

SURPLUS (<u>suhr</u> pluhs) *n.*
excess
Synonyms: glut, superfluity, plethora, repletion, surfeit

COQUETRY (<u>koh</u> keh tree) (koh <u>keh</u> tree) *n.*
flirtation, enticement
Synonyms: seduction, teasing, dalliance

FLORID (<u>flohr</u> ihd) (<u>flahr</u> ihd) *adj.*
gaudy, extremely ornate
Synonyms: flamboyant, ostentatious, loud, garish

those of his own blood, or those whom he had known the longest. His affections, like ivy, were the growth of time; they implied no <u>aptness</u> in the object. Hence, no doubt, the bond that united him to Mr. Richard Enfield, his distant kinsman, the well-known man about town. It was a nut to crack for many, what these two could see in each other, or what subject they could find in common. It was reported by those who encountered them in their Sunday walks that they said nothing, looked **singularly** dull, and would hail with obvious relief the appearance of a friend. For all that, the two men put the greatest store by these excursions, counted them the chief jewel of each week, and not only set aside occasions of pleasure, but even resisted the calls of business, so that they might enjoy them uninterrupted.

It chanced on one of these rambles that their way led them down a by-street in a busy quarter of London. The street was small and what is called quiet, but it drove a thriving trade on the weekdays. The inhabitants were all doing well, it seemed, and all <u>emulously</u> hoping to do better still. They lay out the **surplus** of their gains in **coquetry**; so that the shop fronts stood along that thoroughfare with an air of invitation, like rows of smiling saleswomen. Even on Sunday, when it veiled its more **florid** charms and lay comparatively empty of passage, the street shone out in contrast to its dingy neighbourhood like a fire in a forest; and with its freshly painted shutters, well-polished brasses, and general cleanliness and gaiety of note, instantly caught and pleased the eye of the passenger.

Two doors from one corner, on the left hand going east, the line was broken by the entry of a court, and just at that point, a certain sinister block of building thrust forward its gable on the street. It was two storeys high and showed no window—nothing but a door on the lower storey and a blind forehead of discoloured

SORDID (<u>sohr</u> dihd) *adj.*
    filthy; contemptible and corrupt
        Synonyms: dirty, foul, squalid; wretched,
        degraded, sleazy

NEGLIGENCE (<u>nehg</u> lih jehnts) *n.*
    carelessness, lack of attention
        Synonyms: dereliction, disregard, apathy

RAVAGE (<u>raa</u> vehj) *n.*
    an act of destruction or devastation
        Synonyms: damage, mutilation, desolation

AFFIRMATIVE (uh <u>fihrm</u> uh tihv) *n.*
    a positive response, such as "yes," or a statement of
    agreement
        Synonyms: assertively, decidedly

wall on the upper—and bore in every feature the marks of prolonged and **sordid negligence**. The door, which was equipped with neither bell nor knocker, was blistered and <u>distained</u>. Tramps slouched into the recess and struck matches on the panels, children kept shop upon the steps, the schoolboy had tried his knife on the mouldings, and for close on a generation no one had appeared to drive away these random visitors or to repair their **ravages**.

Mr. Enfield and the lawyer were on the other side of the by-street, but when they came abreast of the entry, the former lifted up his cane and pointed.

"Did you ever <u>remark</u> that door?" he asked. When his companion had replied in the **affirmative**, "It is connected in my mind," added he, "with a very odd story."

"Indeed!" said Mr. Utterson with a slight change of voice. "And what was that?"

"Well, it was this way," returned Mr. Enfield. "I was coming home from some place at the end of the world, about three o'clock of a black winter morning, and my way lay through a part of town where there was literally nothing to be seen but lamps. Street after street, and all the folks asleep—street after street, all lighted up as if for a procession, and all as empty as a church—till at last I got into that state of mind when a man listens and listens and begins to long for the sight of a policeman. All at once, I saw two figures: one a little man who was stumping along eastward at a good walk, and the other a girl of maybe eight or ten who was running as hard as she was able down a cross-street. Well, sir, the two ran into each other naturally enough at the corner, and then came the horrible part of the thing, for the man trampled calmly over the child's body and left her screaming on the ground. It sounds nothing to hear, but it was hellish to see. It wasn't like a man; it was like some damned <u>juggernaut</u>. I gave a view <u>halloa</u>, took to my

LOATHING (<u>loh</u> thihng) *n.*
   feeling of hatred or contempt
      Synonyms: detestation, condemnation

heels, collared my gentleman, and brought him back to where there was already quite a group about the screaming child. He was perfectly cool and made no resistance, but gave me one look, so ugly that it brought out the sweat on me like running. The people who had turned out were the girl's own family; and pretty soon the doctor, for whom she had been sent, put in his appearance.

"Well, the child was not much the worse more frightened, according to the Sawbones, and there, you might have supposed, would be an end to it. But there was one curious circumstance. I had taken a **loathing** to my gentleman at first sight. So had the child's family, which was only natural. But the doctor's case was what struck me. He was the usual cut-and-dry <u>apothecary</u>, of no particular age and colour, with a strong Edinburgh accent, and about as emotional as a bagpipe. Well, sir, he was like the rest of us. Every time he looked at my prisoner, I saw that Sawbones turned sick and white with the desire to kill him. I knew what was in his mind, just as he knew what was in mine, and killing being out of the question, we did the next best. We told the man we could and would make such a scandal out of this as should make his name stink from one end of London to the other. If he had any friends or any credit, we undertook that he should lose them.

"And all the time, as we were pitching it in red-hot, we were keeping the women off him as best we could, for they were as wild as <u>harpies</u>. I never saw a circle of such hateful faces. And there was the man in the middle, with a kind of black sneering coolness—frightened too, I could see that—but carrying it off, sir, really like Satan. 'If you choose to make capital out of this accident,' said he, 'I am naturally helpless. No gentleman but wishes to avoid a scene. Name your figure.' Well, we screwed him up to a hundred pounds for the child's family. He would have clearly liked to stick out, but

APOCRYPHAL (uh <u>pahk</u> ruh fuhl) *adj.*
not genuine, of doubtful authenticity
    Synonyms: erroneous, fictitious, fraudulent, false

there was something about the lot of us that meant mischief, and at last he struck. The next thing was to get the money, and where do you think he carried us but to that place with the door? He whipped out a key, went in, and presently came back with the matter of ten pounds in gold and a cheque for the balance on Coutts's, drawn payable to bearer and signed with a name that I can't mention, though it's one of the points of my story, but it was a name at least very well known and often printed. The figure was stiff, but the signature was good for more than that, if it was only genuine. I took the liberty of pointing out to my gentleman that the whole business looked **apocryphal**, and that a man does not, in real life, walk into a cellar door at four in the morning and come out of it with another man's cheque for close upon a hundred pounds.

"But he was quite easy and sneering. 'Set your mind at rest,' says he. 'I will stay with you till the banks open and cash the cheque myself.' So we all set off, the doctor, and the child's father, and our friend and myself passed the rest of the night in my chambers, and next day, when we had breakfasted, went in a body to the bank. I gave in the cheque myself, and said I had every reason to believe it was a forgery. Not a bit of it. The cheque was genuine."

"Tut-tut!" said Mr. Utterson.

"I see you feel as I do," said Mr. Enfield. "Yes, it's a bad story. For my man was a fellow that nobody could have to do with, a really damnable man, and the person that drew the cheque is the very pink of the proprieties, celebrated too, and (what makes it worse) one of your fellows who do what they call good. Blackmail, I suppose, an honest man paying through the nose for some of the capers of his youth. Blackmail House is what I call that place with the door, in consequence. Though even that, you know, is far from explaining all," he added, and with the words fell into a vein of musing.

From this he was recalled by Mr. Utterson asking rather suddenly, "And you don't know if the drawer of the cheque lives there?"

"A likely place, isn't it?" returned Mr. Enfield. "But I happen to have noticed his address. He lives in some square or other."

"And you never asked about—the place with the door?" said Mr. Utterson.

"No, sir. I had a delicacy," was the reply. "I feel very strongly about putting questions; it partakes too much of the style of the day of judgment. You start a question, and it's like starting a stone. You sit quietly on the top of a hill, and away the stone goes, starting others, and presently some bland old bird (the last you would have thought of) is knocked on the head in his own back garden, and the family have to change their name. No, sir, I make it a rule of mine: the more it looks like Queer Street, the less I ask."

"A very good rule, too," said the lawyer.

"But I have studied the place for myself," continued Mr. Enfield. "It seems scarcely a house. There is no other door, and nobody goes in or out of that one but once in a great while, the gentleman of my adventure. There are three windows looking on the court on the first floor and none below. The windows are always shut, but they're clean. And then there is a chimney, which is generally smoking, so somebody must live there. And yet it's not so sure, for the buildings are so packed together about that court that it's hard to say where one ends and another begins."

The pair walked on again for a while in silence and then, "Enfield," said Mr. Utterson, "that's a good rule of yours."

"Yes, I think it is," returned Enfield.

"But for all that," continued the lawyer, "there's one point I want to ask. I want to ask the name of that man who walked over the child."

DETESTABLE (dee <u>tehst</u> uh buhl) *adj.*
deserving of intense and violent hatred
Synonyms: disgusting, despicable, loathsome

DEFORMED (dih <u>fohrmd</u>) *adj.*
disfigured, spoiled
Synonyms: contorted, twisted, marred, misshapen

DEFORMITY (dih <u>fohr</u> mih tee) *n.*
disfigurement
Synonyms: malformation, disproportion

SULLENNESS (<u>suh</u> luhn nehs) *n.*
gloom, dreariness
Synonyms: moroseness, sulkiness, glumness

PEDANTICALLY (peh <u>daan</u> tih klee) *adv.*
academically; precisely
Synonyms: scholarly, bookishly; particularly

"Well," said Mr. Enfield, "I can't see what harm it would do. It was a man of the name of Hyde."

"Hmm," said Mr. Utterson. "What sort of a man is he to see?"

"He is not easy to describe. There is something wrong with his appearance—something displeasing, something downright **detestable**. I never saw a man I so disliked, and yet I scarce know why. He must be **deformed** somewhere; he gives a strong feeling of **deformity**, although I couldn't specify the point. He's an extraordinary-looking man, and yet I really can name nothing out of the way. No, sir, I can make no hand of it. I can't describe him. And it's not want of memory, for I declare I can see him this moment."

Mr. Utterson again walked some way in silence, and obviously under a weight of consideration. "You are sure he used a key?" he inquired at last.

"My dear sir . . ." began Enfield, surprised out of himself.

"Yes, I know," said Utterson. "I know it must seem strange. The fact is, if I do not ask you the name of the other party, it is because I know it already. You see, Richard, your tale has gone home. If you have been inexact in any point, you had better correct it."

"I think you might have warned me," returned the other, with a touch of **sullenness**. "But I have been **pedantically** exact, as you call it. The fellow had a key, and, what's more, he has it still. I saw him use it not a week ago."

Mr. Utterson sighed deeply but said never a word, and the young man presently resumed. "Here is another lesson to say nothing," said he. "I am ashamed of my long tongue. Let us make a bargain never to refer to this again."

"With all my heart," said the lawyer. "I shake hands on that, Richard."

SOMBER (<u>sahm</u> buhr) *adj.*
melancholy, dismal, dark and gloomy
Synonyms: serious, grave, mournful, lugubrious, funereal

RELISH (<u>reh</u> lihsh) *n.*
an appetite; deep appreciation or enjoyment
Synonyms: hunger; love, fancy, liking, zest, pleasure

DIVINITY (dih <u>vihn</u> ih tee) *n.*
the study of religion; a supreme being, a god
Synonyms: theology; deity, immortal

SOBERLY (<u>soh</u> buhr lee) *adv.*
in a self-controlled manner; seriously; not in a drunken manner
Synonyms: sedately; gravely; dryly

BENEFACTOR (<u>behn</u> uh faak tohr) *n.*
someone giving aid or money
Synonyms: contributor, backer, donor, patron

OBLIGATION (ah blih <u>gay</u> shuhn) *n.*
a sense of duty or promise; a requirement or force to obey
Synonyms: responsibility; constraint, bind, committment

INDIGNATION (ihn dihg <u>nay</u> shun) *n.*
anger caused by something mean or unjust
Synonyms: fury, ire, wrath

Search for Mr. Hyde

That evening Mr. Utterson came home to his bachelor house in **somber** spirits and sat down to dinner without **relish**. It was his custom of a Sunday, when this meal was over, to sit close by the fire, a volume of some dry **divinity** on his reading-desk, until the clock of the neighbouring church rang out the hour of twelve, when he would go **soberly** and gratefully to bed. On this night, however, as soon as the cloth was taken away, he took up a candle and went into his business room. There he opened his safe, took from the most private part of it a document endorsed on the envelope as Dr. Jekyll's Will, and sat down with a clouded brow to study its contents.

The will was <u>holograph,</u> for Mr. Utterson, though he took charge of it now that it was made, had refused to lend the least assistance in the making of it. It provided not only that, in case of the decease of Henry Jekyll, M.D., D.C.L., LL.D., F.R.S., & c., all his possessions were to pass into the hands of his "friend and **benefactor** Edward Hyde," but that in case of Dr. Jekyll's "disappearance or unexplained absence for any period exceeding three calendar months," the said Edward Hyde should step into the said Henry Jekyll's shoes without further delay, and free from any burthen or **obligation**, beyond the payment of a few small sums to the members of the doctor's household. This document had long been the lawyer's eyesore. It offended him both as a lawyer and as a lover of the sane and customary sides of life, to whom the fanciful was the immodest. And hitherto it was his ignorance of Mr. Hyde that had swelled his **indignation**. Now, by a sudden turn, it was his knowledge. It was already bad enough when the

DETESTABLE (dee <u>tehst</u> uh buhl) *adj.*
   deserving of intense and violent hatred
      Synonyms: disgusting, despicable, loathsome

INSUBSTANTIAL (ihn suhb <u>staan</u> shuhl) *adj.*
   small in size or amount; weak, lacking substance
      Synonyms: slight, puny, thin; feeble, infirm

CITADEL (<u>sih</u> tih dehl) *n.*
   a fortress which provides safety and where
   commands are delegated, the center of control
      Synonyms: stronghold, castle, station, support

SOLEMN (<u>sah</u> luhm) *adj.*
   quiet, deeply serious; somberly impressive
      Synonyms: earnest, brooding; dignified, ceremonial

BOISTEROUS (<u>boy</u> stuhr uhs) (<u>boy</u> struhs) *adj.*
   rowdy, loud, unrestrained
      Synonyms: clamorous, uproarious

GENIALITY (jee nee <u>aal</u> ih tee) *n.*
   friendliness, amiability
      Synonyms: warmth, cheerfulness, kindness

REPOSE (rih <u>pohz</u>) *v.* **-ing,-ed.**
   1. to be supported, to place (trust) or to count on
      Synonyms: depend, entrust, invest
   2. to relax or rest; to lie dead
      Synonyms: sleep, slumber

name was but a name of which he could learn no more. It was worse when it began to be clothed upon with **detestable** attributes, and out of the shifting, **insubstantial** mists that had so long baffled his eye, there leaped up the sudden, definite presentment of a fiend.

"I thought it was madness," he said, as he replaced the obnoxious paper in the safe. "And now I begin to fear it is disgrace."

With that he blew out his candle, put on a greatcoat, and set forth in the direction of Cavendish Square, that **citadel** of medicine, where his friend the great Dr. Lanyon had his house and received his crowding patients. If anyone knows, it will be Lanyon, he had thought.

The **solemn** butler knew and welcomed him. He was subjected to no stage of delay, but ushered direct from the door to the dining room, where Dr. Lanyon sat alone over his wine. This was a hearty, healthy, dapper, red-faced gentleman, with a shock of hair prematurely white and a **boisterous** and decided manner. At sight of Mr. Utterson, he sprang up from his chair and welcomed him with both hands. The **geniality**, as was the way of the man, was somewhat theatrical to the eye, but it **reposed** on genuine feeling. For these two were old friends, old mates both at school and college, both thorough respecters of themselves and of each other, and what does not always follow, men who thoroughly enjoyed each other's company.

After a little rambling talk, the lawyer led up to the subject which so disagreeably preoccupied his mind.

"I suppose, Lanyon," he said, "you and I must be the two oldest friends that Henry Jekyll has?"

"I wish the friends were younger," chuckled Dr. Lanyon. "But I suppose we are. And what of that? I see little of him now."

"Indeed!" said Utterson. "I thought you had a bond of common interest."

SAT VOCABULARY

BALDERDASH (<u>bahl</u> duhr daash) *n.*
nonsense
Synonyms: gibberish, rigmarole, tomfoolery, baloney

ESTRANGE (ih <u>straynj</u>) *v.* **-ing,-ed.**
to alienate, keep at a distance
Synonyms: disaffect, separate, divorce

BESIEGE (bih <u>seej</u>) *v.* **-ing,-ed.**
to press with requests; to cause worry or distress; to
surround with armed forces
Synonyms: bombard, harass; hurt; block, confine

NOCTURNAL (nok <u>tuhr</u> nuhl) *adj.*
pertaining to night, active at night
Synonyms: nightly, dark

"We had," was his reply. "But it is more than ten years since Henry Jekyll became too fanciful for me. He began to go wrong, wrong in mind. And though, of course, I continue to take an interest in him for old sake's sake as they say, I see and I have seen devilishly little of the man. Such unscientific **balderdash**," added the doctor, flushing suddenly purple, "would have **estranged** Damon and Pythias."

This little spurt of temper was somewhat of a relief to Mr. Utterson. They have only differed on some point of science, he thought, and being a man of no scientific passions (except in the matter of <u>conveyancing</u>), he even added, It is nothing worse than that! He gave his friend a few seconds to recover his composure, and then approached the question he had come to put.

"Did you ever come across a <u>protégé</u> of his—one Hyde?" he asked.

"Hyde?" repeated Lanyon. "No. Never heard of him. Since my time."

That was the amount of information that the lawyer carried back with him to the great, dark bed on which he tossed to and fro until the small hours of the morning began to grow large. It was a night of little ease to his toiling mind, toiling in mere darkness and **besieged** by questions.

Six o'clock struck on the bells of the church that was so conveniently near to Mr. Utterson's dwelling, and still he was digging at the problem. Hitherto it had touched him on the intellectual side alone, but now his imagination also was engaged, or rather enslaved, and as he lay and tossed in the gross darkness of the night and the curtained room, Mr. Enfield's tale went by before his mind in a scroll of lighted pictures. He would be aware of the great field of lamps of a **nocturnal** city, then of the figure of a man walking swiftly, then of a child running from the doctor's, and then these met, and that human

STEALTHILY (<u>stehl</u> thuh lee) *adv.*
quietly and cautiously
Synonyms: furtively, secretly, surreptitiously, covertly

LABYRINTH (<u>laab</u> uh rihnth) *n.*
maze
Synonyms: entanglement, mesh, web

SINGULARLY (<u>sihn</u> gyuh luhr lee) *adv.*
uncommonly, peculiarly
Synonyms: unusually, oddly, rarely, uniquely

SOLITUDE (<u>sahl</u> ih tood) *n.*
social isolation; time spent alone
Synonyms: seclusion, withdrawal, retirement; loneliness

CONCOURSE (<u>kahn</u> kohrs) *n.*
an act of coming together; a large open space where crowds gather or pass
Synonyms: confluence, assembly, meeting; plaza

juggernaut trod the child down and passed on regardless of her screams. Or else he would see a room in a rich house, where his friend lay asleep, dreaming and smiling at his dreams. And then the door of that room would be opened, the curtains of the bed plucked apart, the sleeper recalled, and, lo! There would stand by his side a figure to whom power was given, and even at that dead hour he must rise and do its bidding. The figure in these two phases haunted the lawyer all night, and if at any time he dozed over, it was but to see it glide more **stealthily** through sleeping houses, or move the more swiftly, and still the more swiftly, even to dizziness, through wider **labyrinths** of lamp-lighted city, and at every street corner crush a child and leave her screaming. And still the figure had no face by which he might know it. Even in his dreams it had no face, or one that baffled him and melted before his eyes. And thus it was that there sprang up and grew apace in the lawyer's mind a **singularly** strong, almost an inordinate curiosity to behold the features of the real Mr. Hyde. If he could but once set eyes on him, he thought the mystery would lighten and perhaps roll altogether away, as was the habit of mysterious things when well examined. He might see a reason for his friend's strange preference or bondage (call it which you please), and even for the startling clauses of the will. And at least it would be a face worth seeing: the face of a man who was without bowels of mercy, a face which had but to show itself to raise up, in the mind of the <u>unimpressionable</u> Enfield, a spirit of enduring hatred.

From that time forward, Mr. Utterson began to haunt the door in the by-street of shops. In the morning before office hours, at noon when business was plenty and time scarce, at night under the face of the fogged city moon. By all lights and at all hours of **solitude** or **concourse**, the lawyer was to be found on his chosen post. If he be Mr. Hyde, he had thought, I shall be Mr. Seek.

AUDIBLE (<u>aw</u> dih buhl) *adj.*
capable of being heard
    Synonyms: detectable, perceptible

DRAW *v.* **-ing, drew, drawn.**
    1. to move steadily
        Synonyms: proceed, continue, progress
    2. to pull, drag; to attract
        Synonyms: haul, tow, lug; lure, entice

INCLINATION (ihn cluh <u>nay</u> shuhn) *n.*
tendency toward
    Synonyms: trend, preference, disposition,
propensity

And at last his patience was rewarded. It was a fine dry night, frost in the air, the streets as clean as a ballroom floor, the lamps, unshaken by any wind, drawing a regular pattern of light and shadow. By ten o'clock, when the shops were closed, the by-street was very solitary and, in spite of the low growl of London from all around, very silent. Small sounds carried far, domestic sounds out of the houses were clearly **audible** on either side of the roadway, and the rumour of the approach of any passenger preceded him by a long time. Mr. Utterson had been some minutes at his post when he was aware of an odd light footstep **drawing** near. In the course of his nightly patrols he had long grown accustomed to the quaint effect with which the footfalls of a single person, while he is still a great way off, suddenly spring out distinct from the vast hum and clatter of the city. Yet his attention had never before been so sharply and decisively arrested, and it was with a strong, superstitious pre-vision of success that he withdrew into the entry of the court.

The steps **drew** swiftly nearer and swelled out suddenly louder as they turned the end of the street. The lawyer, looking forth from the entry, could soon see what manner of man he had to deal with. He was small and very plainly dressed, and the look of him, even at that distance, went somehow strongly against the watcher's **inclination**. But he made straight for the door, crossing the roadway to save time, and as he came, he **drew** a key from his pocket, like one approaching home.

Mr. Utterson stepped out and touched him on the shoulder as he passed. "Mr. Hyde, I think?"

Mr. Hyde shrank back with a hissing intake of the breath. But his fear was only momentary, and though he did not look the lawyer in the face, he answered coolly enough, "That is my name. What do you want?"

"I see you are going in," returned the lawyer. "I am an old friend of Dr. Jekyll's—Mr. Utterson, of Gaunt Street—you must have heard my name. And meeting you so conveniently, I thought you might admit me."

"You will not find Dr. Jekyll; he is from home," replied Mr. Hyde, blowing in the key. And then suddenly, but still without looking up, "How did you know me?" he asked.

"On your side," said Mr. Utterson, "will you do me a favour?"

"With pleasure," replied the other. "What shall it be?"

"Will you let me see your face?" asked the lawyer.

Mr. Hyde appeared to hesitate, and then, as if upon some sudden reflection, fronted about with an air of defiance; and the pair stared at each other pretty fixedly for a few seconds. "Now I shall know you again," said Mr. Utterson. "It may be useful."

"Yes," returned Mr. Hyde, "it is as well we have met, and à propos, you should have my address." And he gave a number of a street in Soho.

Good God! thought Mr. Utterson, can he too have been thinking of the will? But he kept his feelings to himself and only grunted in acknowledgment of the address.

"And now," said the other, "how did you know me?"

"By description," was the reply.

"Whose description?"

"We have common friends," said Mr. Utterson.

"Common friends!" echoed Mr. Hyde, a little hoarsely. "Who are they?"

"Jekyll, for instance," said the lawyer.

"He never told you," cried Mr. Hyde with a flush of anger. "I did not think you would have lied."

"Come," said Mr. Utterson, "that is not fitting language."

The other snarled aloud into a savage laugh, and the

DISQUIETUDE (dihs <u>kwie</u> eh tood) *n.*
anxiety, lack of peace or tranquility
Synonyms: edginess, uneasiness

PERPLEXITY (puhr <u>plek</u> sih tee) *n.*
the state of being puzzled or confused
Synonyms: bewilderment, distraction, disorientation

DEFORMITY (dih <u>fohr</u> mih tee) *n.*
disfigurement
Synonyms: malformation, disproportion

TIMIDITY (tih <u>mih</u> dih tee) *n.*
shyness, fearfulness of the unfamiliar
Synonyms: bashfulness, hesitancy, insecurity

LOATHING (<u>loh</u> thihng) *n.*
feeling of hatred or contempt
Synonyms: detestation, condemnation

PERPLEXED (puhr <u>plekst</u>) *adj.*
puzzled or confused
Synonyms: bewildered, distracted, disoriented

TRANSPIRE (traan <u>spie</u> uhr) *v.* **-ing,-ed.**
1. to give off, like a vapor
Synonyms: excrete, evaporate
2. to happen, occur; to become known
Synonyms: befall, betide; emerge, come out

OBSCURE (uhb <u>skyoor</u>) *adj.*
not well known; dim, unclear
Synonyms: remote, minor; dark, faint

next moment, with extraordinary quickness, he had unlocked the door and disappeared into the house.

The lawyer stood awhile when Mr. Hyde had left him, the picture of **disquietude**. Then he began slowly to mount the street, pausing every step or two and putting his hand to his brow like a man in mental **perplexity**. The problem he was thus debating as he walked was one of a class that is rarely solved. Mr. Hyde was pale and dwarfish. He gave an impression of **deformity** without any nameable malformation, he had a displeasing smile, he had borne himself to the lawyer with a sort of murderous mixture of **timidity** and boldness, and he spoke with a husky, whispering and somewhat broken voice. All these were points against him, but not all of these together could explain the hitherto unknown disgust, **loathing**, and fear with which Mr. Utterson regarded him.

"There must be something else," said the **perplexed** gentleman. "There *is* something more, if I could find a name for it. God bless me, the man seems hardly human! Something <u>troglodytic</u>, shall we say? Or can it be the old story of Dr. Fell? Or is it the mere radiance of a foul soul that thus **transpires** through, and transfigures, its clay continent? The last, I think, for, oh my poor old Harry Jekyll, if ever I read Satan's signature upon a face, it is on that of your new friend!"

Round the corner from the by-street there was a square of ancient, handsome houses, now for the most part decayed from their high estate, and let in flats and chambers to all sorts and conditions of men: map engravers, architects, shady lawyers, and the agents of **obscure** enterprises. One house, however, second from the corner, was still occupied entire, and at the door of this, which wore a great air of wealth and comfort though it was now plunged in darkness except for the fan-light, Mr. Utterson stopped and knocked. A well-dressed, elderly servant opened the door.

DRAW *v.* **-ing, drew, drawn.**
1. to move steadily
   Synonyms: proceed, continue, progress
2. to pull, drag; to attract
   Synonyms: haul, tow, lug; lure, entice

REPOSE (rih <u>pohz</u>) *v.* **-ing,-ed.**
1. to place (trust) or to count on, to be supported by
   Synonyms: entrust, invest, depend
2. to relax or rest; to lie dead
   Synonyms: sleep, slumber

DR. JEKYLL AND MR. HYDE

"Is Dr. Jekyll at home, Poole?" asked the lawyer.

"I will see, Mr. Utterson," said Poole, admitting the visitor, as he spoke, into a large, low-roofed, comfortable hall, paved with flags, warmed (after the fashion of a country house) by a bright, open fire, and furnished with costly cabinets of oak. "Will you wait here by the fire, sir? Or shall I give you a light in the dining room?"

"Here, thank you," said the lawyer, and he **drew** near and leaned on the tall fender. This hall in which he was now left alone was a pet fancy of his friend the doctor's, and Utterson himself was wont to speak of it as the pleasantest room in London. But tonight there was a shudder in his blood. The face of Hyde sat heavy on his memory. He felt (what was rare in him) a nausea and distaste of life, and in the gloom of his spirits, he seemed to read a menace in the flickering of the firelight on the polished cabinets and the uneasy starting of the shadow on the roof. He was ashamed of his relief when Poole presently returned to announce that Dr. Jekyll was gone out.

"I saw Mr. Hyde go in by the old dissecting-room door, Poole," he said. "Is that right, when Dr. Jekyll is from home?"

"Quite right, Mr. Utterson, sir," replied the servant. "Mr. Hyde has a key."

"Your master seems to **repose** a great deal of trust in that young man, Poole," resumed the other, musingly.

"Yes, sir, he do indeed," said Poole. "We all have orders to obey him."

"I do not think I ever met Mr. Hyde?" asked Utterson.

"Oh dear no, sir. He never *dines* here," replied the butler. "Indeed, we see very little of him on this side of the house. He mostly comes and goes by the laboratory."

"Well, good-night, Poole."

MISGIVE (mihs <u>gihv</u>) *v.* **-ing,-gave.**
to be suspicious or doubtful, to sense foreboding
Synonyms: distrust, skepticize, disbelieve

CONDONE (kuhn <u>dohn</u>) *v.* **-ing,-ed.**
to pardon or forgive; overlook, justify, or excuse a
fault
Synonyms: vindicate, dismiss; defend

BROOD *v.* **-ing,-ed.**
to think about in a gloomy or serious way
Synonyms: ponder, worry, obsess

INIQUITY (ih <u>nihk</u> wih tee) *n.*
sin, evil act
Synonyms: immorality, injustice, wickedness, vice

APPREHENSION (aa prih <u>hehn</u> shuhn) *n.*
suspicion or fear of future or unknown evil; the act
of perceiving or comprehending; a legal seizure
Synonyms: concern, worry; understanding;
capture

SOBER (<u>soh</u> buhr) *adj.*
serious; plain or self-controlled; not intoxicated
Synonyms: grave; subdued, sedate; dry, not drunk

"Good-night, Mr. Utterson."

And the lawyer set out homeward with a very heavy heart. Poor Harry Jekyll, he thought. My mind **misgives** me; he is in deep waters! He was wild when he was young—a long while ago—to be sure; but in the law of God there is no statute of limitations. Ah, it must be that, the ghost of some old sin, the cancer of some concealed disgrace, punishment coming, _pede claudo_, years after memory has forgotten and self-love **condoned** the fault. And the lawyer, scared by the thought, **brooded** awhile on his own past, groping in all the corners of memory, lest by chance some jack-in-the-box of an old **iniquity** should leap to light there. His past was fairly blameless—few men could read the rolls of their life with less **apprehension**—yet he was humbled to the dust by the many ill things he had done, and raised up again into a **sober** and fearful gratitude by the many that he had come so near to doing, yet avoided. And then by a return on his former subject, he conceived a spark of hope. This Master Hyde, if he were studied, thought he, must have secrets of his own. Black secrets, by the look of him, secrets compared to which poor Jekyll's worst would be like sunshine. Things cannot continue as they are. It turns me quite cold to think of this creature stealing like a thief to Harry's bedside. Poor Harry, what a wakening! And the danger of it, for if this Hyde suspects the existence of the will, he may grow impatient to inherit. Ay, I must put my shoulder to the wheel—if Jekyll will but let me, he added, if Jekyll will only let me. For once more he saw before his mind's eye, as clear as a transparency, the strange clauses of the will.

CONTRIVE (kuhn <u>triev</u>) *v.* **-ing,-ed.**
to devise, plan, or manage; to form in an artistic manner
Synonyms: concoct, scheme; create, design

SCORE (skohr) *n.*
1. a very large number
Synonyms: many, multitude
2. a notch or scratch, made to keep tally
Synonyms: furrow, scrape, groove

DETAIN (dih <u>tayn</u>) (dee <u>tayn</u>) *v.* **-ing,-ed.**
to restrain from continuing on; to hold
Synonyms: delay, inhibit; apprehend, keep

UNOBTRUSIVE (uhn uhb <u>troo</u> sihv) *adj.*
low-key and humble
Synonyms: modest, reserved, subdued

SOLITUDE (<u>sahl</u> ih tood) *n.*
social isolation; time spent alone
Synonyms: seclusion, withdrawal, retirement; loneliness

SOBER (<u>soh</u> buhr) *v.* **-ing,-ed.**
to make not intoxicated; to become self-controlled or serious
Synonyms: abstain; subdue, sedate

PEDANT (<u>peh</u> daant) *n.*
an uninspired, boring academic
Synonyms: scholar, schoolmaster, pedagogue

BLATANT (<u>blay</u> tihnt) *adj.*
glaring, obvious, showy
Synonyms: conspicuous, egregious, flagrant

DR. JEKYLL WAS QUITE AT EASE

A <u>fortnight</u> later, by excellent good fortune, the doctor gave one of his pleasant dinners to some five or six old cronies, all intelligent, <u>reputable</u> men and all judges of good wine, and Mr. Utterson so **contrived** that he remained behind after the others had departed. This was no new arrangement, but a thing that had befallen many **scores** of times. Where Utterson was liked, he was liked well. Hosts loved to **detain** the dry lawyer, when the light-hearted and the loose-tongued had already their foot on the threshold. They liked to sit awhile in his **unobtrusive** company, practising for **solitude**, **sobering** their minds in the man's rich silence, after the expense and strain of gaiety. To this rule Dr. Jekyll was no exception, and as he now sat on the opposite side of the fire—a large, well-made, smooth-faced man of fifty, with something of a slyish cast perhaps, but every mark of capacity and kindness—you could see by his looks that he cherished for Mr. Utterson a sincere and warm affection.

"I have been wanting to speak to you, Jekyll," began the latter. "You know that will of yours?"

A close observer might have gathered that the topic was distasteful, but the doctor carried it off gaily. "My poor Utterson," said he, "you are unfortunate in such a client. I never saw a man so distressed as you were by my will, unless it were that hide-bound **pedant**, Lanyon, at what he called my scientific <u>heresies</u>. Oh, I know he's a good fellow—you needn't frown—an excellent fellow, and I always mean to see more of him, but a hide-bound **pedant** for all that, an ignorant, **blatant**

SAT VOCABULARY

PEDANT (<u>peh</u> daant) *n.*
an uninspired, boring academic
Synonyms: scholar, schoolmaster, pedagogue

TRIFLE (<u>trie</u> fuhl) *n.*
a slight degree or small amount; something of slight
worth or little importance
Synonyms: bit, speck, fraction, trace, dash;
triviality, novelty, trinket, bit

ABOMINABLE (uh <u>bah</u> mihn uh buhl) *adj.*
loathsome, detestable
Synonyms: abhorrent, terrible, beastly, deplorable

INCOHERENCY (ihn koh <u>hihr</u> uhn see) *n.*
the inability to think or express one's thoughts in a
clear or orderly manner
Synonyms: unintelligibility, confusion, disarray

pedant. I was never more disappointed in any man than Lanyon."

"You know I never approved of it," pursued Utterson, ruthlessly disregarding the fresh topic.

"My will? Yes, certainly, I know that," said the doctor, a **trifle** sharply. "You have told me so."

"Well, I tell you so again," continued the lawyer. "I have been learning something of young Hyde."

The large handsome face of Dr. Jekyll grew pale to the very lips, and there came a blackness about his eyes. "I do not care to hear more," said he. "This is a matter I thought we had agreed to drop."

"What I heard was **abominable**," said Utterson.

"It can make no change. You do not understand my position," returned the doctor, with a certain **incoherency** of manner. "I am painfully situated, Utterson. My position is a very strange—a very strange one. It is one of those affairs that cannot be mended by talking."

"Jekyll," said Utterson, "you know me. I am a man to be trusted. Make a clean breast of this in confidence, and I make no doubt I can get you out of it."

"My good Utterson," said the doctor, "this is very good of you, this is downright good of you, and I cannot find words to thank you in. I believe you fully; I would trust you before any man alive, ay, before myself, if I could make the choice. But indeed it isn't what you fancy. It is not so bad as that; and just to put your good heart at rest, I will tell you one thing: the moment I choose, I can be rid of Mr. Hyde. I give you my hand upon that, and I thank you again and again. And I will just add one little word, Utterson, that I'm sure you'll take in good part. This is a private matter, and I beg of you to let it sleep."

Utterson reflected a little, looking in the fire.

SAT VOCABULARY

"I have no doubt you are perfectly right," he said at last, getting to his feet.

"Well, but since we have touched upon this business, and for the last time, I hope," continued the doctor, "there is one point I should like you to understand. I have really a very great interest in poor Hyde. I know you have seen him. He told me so, and I fear he was rude. But I do sincerely take a great, a very great interest in that young man, and if I am taken away, Utterson, I wish you to promise me that you will bear with him and get his rights for him. I think you would, if you knew all, and it would be a weight off my mind if you would promise."

"I can't pretend that I shall ever like him," said the lawyer.

"I don't ask that," pleaded Jekyll, laying his hand upon the other's arm. "I only ask for justice. I only ask you to help him for my sake, when I am no longer here."

Utterson heaved an irrepressible sigh. "Well," said he, "I promise."

SINGULAR (<u>sihn</u> gyuh luhr) *adj.*
 uncommon, peculiar
  Synonyms: unusual, odd, rare, unique, individual

FEROCITY (fuhr <u>ah</u> sih tee) *n.*
 fierceness, violence
  Synonyms: fury, wildness, vehemence, turbulence

DRAW *v.* **-ing, drew, drawn.**
 1. to move steadily
  Synonyms: proceed, continue, progress
 2. to pull, drag; to attract
  Synonyms: haul, tow, lug; lure, entice

ACCOST (uh <u>cahst</u>) (uh <u>kawst</u>) *v.* **-ing,-ed.**
 to approach and speak to someone, often in an
 aggressive way
  Synonyms: bother, address, confront

DISPOSITION (dihs puh <u>zih</u> shuhn) *n.*
 mood or temperament
  Synonyms: behavior, tendency, inclination, nature

THE CAREW MURDER CASE

Nearly a year later, in the month of October, 18——, London was startled by a crime of **singular ferocity**, and rendered all the more notable by the high position of the victim. The details were few and startling. A maid-servant living alone in a house not far from the river had gone upstairs to bed about eleven. Although a fog rolled over the city in the small hours, the early part of the night was cloudless, and the lane, which the maid's window overlooked, was brilliantly lit by the full moon. It seems she was romantically given, for she sat down upon her box, which stood immediately under the window, and fell into a dream of musing. Never (she used to say, with streaming tears, when she narrated that experience), never had she felt more at peace with all men or thought more kindly of the world. And as she so sat she became aware of an aged and beautiful gentleman with white hair **drawing** near along the lane, and advancing to meet him, another and very small gentleman, to whom at first she paid less attention. When they had come within speech (which was just under the maid's eyes), the older man bowed and **accosted** the other with a very pretty manner of politeness. It did not seem as if the subject of his address were of great importance. Indeed, from his pointing, it sometimes appeared as if he were only inquiring his way; but the moon shone on his face as he spoke, and the girl was pleased to watch it. It seemed to breathe such an innocent and old-world kindness of **disposition**, yet with something high too, as of a well-founded self-content. Presently her eye wandered to the other, and she was surprised to recognise in him a certain Mr. Hyde, who had once visited her master and for whom she had

TRIFLE (<u>trie</u> fuhl) *v.* **-ing,-ed.**
    to toy around with; to waste time or money
        Synonyms: putter, fidget; squander

TRIFLE (<u>trie</u> fuhl) *adj.*
    to a slight degree or small amount; of slight
    worth or little importance
        Synonyms: bit, speck, fraction, trace, dash

AUDIBLY (<u>aw</u> dih blee) *adv.*
    in a manner capable of being heard, aloud
        Synonyms: detectably, perceptibly, loudly, plainly

INSENSATE (ihn <u>sehn</u> sayt) (ihn <u>sehn</u> siht) *adj.*
    without sense or human feeling; lacking sensation,
    unconscious
        Synonyms: cold-blooded; inanimate, numb

SOLEMN (<u>sah</u> luhm) *adj.*
    quiet, deeply serious; somberly impressive
        Synonyms: earnest, brooding; dignified, ceremonial

COUNTENANCE (<u>kown</u> tuh nuhns) *n.*
    appearance, facial expression
        Synonyms: face, features, visage

conceived a dislike. He had in his hand a heavy cane, with which he was **trifling**, but he answered never a word and seemed to listen with an ill-contained impatience. And then all of a sudden he broke out in a great flame of anger, stamping with his foot, <u>brandishing</u> the cane, and carrying on (as the maid described it) like a madman. The old gentleman took a step back, with the air of one very much surprised and a **trifle** hurt, and at that Mr. Hyde broke out of all bounds, and clubbed him to the earth. And next moment, with apelike fury, he was trampling his victim underfoot and hailing down a storm of blows, under which the bones were **audibly** shattered and the body jumped upon the roadway. At the horror of these sights and sounds, the maid fainted.

It was two o'clock when she came to herself and called for the police. The murderer was gone long ago, but there lay his victim in the middle of the lane, incredibly <u>mangled</u>. The stick with which the deed had been done, although it was of some rare and very tough and heavy wood, had broken in the middle under the stress of this **insensate** cruelty, and one splintered half had rolled in the neighbouring gutter. The other, without doubt, had been carried away by the murderer. A purse and a gold watch were found upon the victim, but no cards or papers, except a sealed and stamped envelope, which he had been probably carrying to the post, and which bore the name and address of Mr. Utterson.

This was brought to the lawyer the next morning, before he was out of bed, and he had no sooner seen it and been told the circumstances than he shot out a **solemn** lip. "I shall say nothing till I have seen the body," said he. "This may be very serious. Have the kindness to wait while I dress." And with the same grave **countenance**, he hurried through his breakfast and drove to the police station, whither the body had been carried. As soon as he came into the cell, he nodded.

LURID (<u>loor</u> ihd) *adj.*
glowing with unnatural redness; harshly shocking,
revolting
Synonyms: shining, glaring; ghastly, garish,
gruesome, grisly, macabre

CONFLAGRATION (kahn fluh <u>gray</u> shuhn) *n.*
a big, destructive fire; an intense scene
Synonyms: blaze, holocaust, inferno; spectacle

KINDLE (<u>kihn</u> duhl) *v.* **-ing,-ed.**
to set fire to or ignite; to excite or inspire
Synonyms: light, spark; arouse, awaken

"Yes," said he, "I recognise him. I am sorry to say that this is Sir Danvers Carew."

"Good God, sir!" exclaimed the officer. "Is it possible?" And the next moment his eye lighted up with professional ambition. "This will make a deal of noise," he said. "And perhaps you can help us to the man." And he briefly narrated what the maid had seen, and showed the broken stick.

Mr. Utterson had already <u>quailed</u> at the name of Hyde, but when the stick was laid before him, he could doubt no longer. Broken and battered as it was, he recognised it for one that he had himself presented many years before to Henry Jekyll.

"Is this Mr. Hyde a person of small stature?" he inquired.

"Particularly small and particularly wicked-looking, is what the maid calls him," said the officer.

Mr. Utterson reflected and then, raising his head, "If you will come with me in my cab," he said, "I think I can take you to his house."

It was by this time about nine in the morning, and the first fog of the season. A great chocolate-coloured <u>pall</u> lowered over heaven, but the wind was continually charging and routing these <u>embattled</u> vapours, so that as the cab crawled from street to street, Mr. Utterson beheld a marvellous number of degrees and hues of twilight. For here it would be dark like the back-end of evening, and there would be a glow of a rich, **lurid** brown, like the light of some strange **conflagration**. And here, for a moment, the fog would be quite broken up, and a <u>haggard</u> shaft of daylight would glance in between the swirling wreaths. The dismal quarter of Soho seen under these changing glimpses, with its muddy ways, and <u>slatternly</u> passengers, and its lamps, which had never been extinguished or had been **kindled** afresh to combat this mournful reinvasion of darkness,

ASSAIL (uh <u>sayl</u>) *v.* **-ing,-ed.**
to attack, assault
Synonyms: beset, storm, strike

DRAW *v.* **-ing, drew, drawn.**
1. to move steadily
Synonyms: proceed, continue, progress
2. to pull, drag; to attract
Synonyms: haul, tow, lug; lure, entice

HYPOCRISY (hih <u>pah</u> krih see) *n.*
the practice of claiming beliefs or virtues that one
doesn't really possess
Synonyms: fraud, falseness, fakeness, lip service

ODIOUS (<u>oh</u> dee uhs) *adj.*
hateful, contemptible
Synonyms: detestable, obnoxious, offensive,
repellent, loathsome

seemed, in the lawyer's eyes, like a district of some city in a nightmare. The thoughts of his mind, besides, were of the gloomiest dye, and when he glanced at the companion of his drive, he was conscious of some touch of that terror of the law and the law's officers which may at times **assail** the most honest.

As the cab **drew** up before the address indicated, the fog lifted a little and showed him a dingy street, a gin palace, a low French eating-house, a shop for the retail of penny numbers and two-penny salads, many ragged children huddled in the doorways, and many women of many different nationalities passing out, key in hand, to have a morning glass; and the next moment the fog settled down again upon that part, as brown as umber, and cut him off from his <u>blackguardly</u> surroundings. This was the home of Henry Jekyll's favourite, of a man who was heir to a quarter of a million sterling.

An ivory-faced and silvery-haired old woman opened the door. She had an evil face, smoothed by **hypocrisy**, but her manners were excellent. Yes, she said, this was Mr. Hyde's, but he was not at home. He had been in that night very late, but had gone away again in less than an hour. There was nothing strange in that; his habits were very irregular, and he was often absent. For instance, it was nearly two months since she had seen him till yesterday.

"Very well then, we wish to see his rooms," said the lawyer, and when the woman began to declare it was impossible, "I had better tell you who this person is," he added. "This is Inspector Newcomen of Scotland Yard."

A flash of **odious** joy appeared upon the woman's face. "Ah!" said she, "He is in trouble! What has he done?"

Mr. Utterson and the inspector exchanged glances. "He don't seem a very popular character," observed the latter. "And now, my good woman, just let me and this gentleman have a look about us."

LUXURY (<u>luhg</u> zhoor ee) *n.*
  something had or done purely for enjoyment
    Synonyms: comfort, indulgence, splendor, frill

DISINTER (dihs ihn <u>tuhr</u>) *v.* **-ring,-red.**
  to bring out into the open; to dig up from a grave
    Synonyms: disclose, reveal; exhume

DEFORMITY (dih <u>fohr</u> mih tee) *n.*
  disfigurement
    Synonyms: malformation, disproportion

In the whole extent of the house, which but for the old woman remained otherwise empty, Mr. Hyde had only used a couple of rooms, but these were furnished with **luxury** and good taste. A closet was filled with wine; the plate was of silver, the <u>napery</u> elegant; a good picture hung upon the walls, a gift (as Utterson supposed) from Henry Jekyll, who was much of a connoisseur; and the carpets were of many piles and agreeable in colour. At this moment, however, the rooms bore every mark of having been recently and hurriedly ransacked. Clothes lay about the floor, with their pockets inside out. Lockfast drawers stood open, and on the hearth there lay a pile of grey ashes, as though many papers had been burned. From these embers the inspector **disinterred** the butt end of a green cheque book, which had resisted the action of the fire. The other half of the stick was found behind the door, and as this clinched his suspicions, the officer declared himself delighted. A visit to the bank, where several thousand pounds were found to be lying to the murderer's credit, completed his gratification.

"You may depend upon it, sir," he told Mr. Utterson. "I have him in my hand. He must have lost his head, or he never would have left the stick or, above all, burned the cheque book. Why, money's life to the man. We have nothing to do but wait for him at the bank, and get out the handbills."

This last, however, was not so easy of accomplishment, for Mr. Hyde had numbered few familiars—even the master of the servant-maid had only seen him twice. His family could nowhere be traced, he had never been photographed, and the few who could describe him differed widely, as common observers will. Only on one point were they agreed, and that was the haunting sense of unexpressed **deformity** with which the fugitive impressed his beholders.

INDIFFERENTLY (ihn <u>dihf</u> ruhnt lee)
(ihn <u>dihf</u> uhr uhnt lee) *adv.*
   in an uncaring manner; without bias
      Synonyms: disinterestedly, apathetically;
      impartially

GAUNT (gawnt) *adj.*
   bleak and barren; thin and bony
      Synonyms: desolate, empty, spare; lean, skinny,
      scrawny, lank

INCIDENT OF THE LETTER

It was late in the afternoon when Mr. Utterson found his way to Dr. Jekyll's door, where he was at once admitted by Poole, and carried down by the kitchen offices and across a yard which had once been a garden, to the building which was **indifferently** known as the laboratory or the dissecting-rooms. The doctor had bought the house from the heirs of a celebrated surgeon, and his own tastes being rather chemical than anatomical, had changed the destination of the block at the bottom of the garden. It was the first time that the lawyer had been received in that part of his friend's quarters; and he eyed the dingy windowless structure with curiosity. He gazed round with a distasteful sense of strangeness as he crossed the theatre, once crowded with eager students and now lying **gaunt** and silent, the tables laden with chemical apparatus, the floor strewn with crates and littered with packing straw, and the light falling dimly through the foggy <u>cupola</u>. At the further end, a flight of stairs mounted to a door covered with red <u>baize,</u> and through this Mr. Utterson was at last received into the doctor's cabinet. It was a large room, fitted round with glass presses, furnished, among other things, with a <u>cheval-glass</u> and a business table, and looking out upon the court by three dusty windows barred with iron. The fire burned in the grate; a lamp was set lighted on the chimney-shelf, for even in the houses the fog began to lie thickly; and there, close up to the warmth, sat Dr. Jekyll, looking deadly sick. He did not rise to meet his visitor, but held out a cold hand and bade him welcome in a changed voice.

RUMINATE (<u>roo</u> muh nayt) *v.* **-ing,-ed.**
to contemplate, reflect upon
  Synonyms: ponder, meditate, deliberate, mull, muse

BENEFACTOR (<u>behn</u> uh faak tohr) *n.*
someone giving aid or money
  Synonyms: contributor, backer, donor, patron

"And now," said Mr. Utterson, as soon as Poole had left them, "you have heard the news?"

The doctor shuddered. "They were crying it in the square," he said. "I heard them in my dining room."

"One word," said the lawyer. "Carew was my client, but so are you; and I want to know what I am doing. You have not been mad enough to hide this fellow?"

"Utterson, I swear to God," cried the doctor, "I swear to God I will never set eyes on him again. I bind my honour to you that I am done with him in this world. It is all at an end. And indeed he does not want my help. You do not know him as I do; he is safe, he is quite safe. mark my words, he will never more be heard of."

The lawyer listened gloomily; he did not like his friend's feverish manner. "You seem pretty sure of him," said he, "and for your sake, I hope you may be right. If it came to a trial, your name might appear."

"I am quite sure of him," replied Jekyll. "I have grounds for certainty that I cannot share with any one. But there is one thing on which you may advise me. I have—I have received a letter, and I am at a loss whether I should show it to the police. I should like to leave it in your hands, Utterson. You would judge wisely, I am sure; I have so great a trust in you."

"You fear, I suppose, that it might lead to his detection?" asked the lawyer.

"No," said the other. "I cannot say that I care what becomes of Hyde. I am quite done with him. I was thinking of my own character, which this hateful business has rather exposed."

Utterson **ruminated** awhile. He was surprised at his friend's selfishness, and yet relieved by it. "Well," said he, at last, "let me see the letter."

The letter was written in an odd, upright hand and signed "Edward Hyde," and it signified, briefly enough, that the writer's **benefactor**, Dr. Jekyll, whom he had

QUALM (kwahlm) *n.*
    a sudden feeling of sickness; a sudden feeling of doubt
        Synonyms: queasiness; worry, scruple, misgiving

SOLEMNLY (<u>sah</u> luhm lee) *adv.*
    seriously or somberly
        Synonyms: quietly, earnestly, ceremonially

long so unworthily repaid for a thousand generosities, need labour under no alarm for his safety as he had means of escape on which he placed a sure dependence. The lawyer liked this letter well enough; it put a better colour on the intimacy than he had looked for, and he blamed himself for some of his past suspicions.

"Have you the envelope?" he asked.

"I burned it," replied Jekyll, "before I thought what it was about. But it bore no postmark. The note was handed in."

"Shall I keep this and sleep upon it?" asked Utterson.

"I wish you to judge for me entirely," was the reply. "I have lost confidence in myself."

"Well, I shall consider," returned the lawyer. "And now one word more. It was Hyde who dictated the terms in your will about that disappearance?"

The doctor seemed seized with a **qualm** of faintness. He shut his mouth tight and nodded.

"I knew it," said Utterson. "He meant to murder you. You have had a fine escape."

"I have had what is far more to the purpose," returned the doctor **solemnly**. "I have had a lesson—oh God, Utterson, what a lesson I have had!" And he covered his face for a moment with his hands.

On his way out, the lawyer stopped and had a word or two with Poole. "By the by," said he, "there was a letter handed in today. What was the messenger like?" But Poole was positive nothing had come except by post, "and only circulars by that," he added.

This news sent off the visitor with his fears renewed. Plainly the letter had come by the laboratory door. Possibly, indeed, it had been written in the cabinet, and if that were so, it must be differently judged, and handled with the more caution. The newsboys, as he went, were crying themselves hoarse along the footways: "Special edition. Shocking murder of an M.P." That was the

ORATION (ohr <u>ay</u> shuhn) *n.*
lecture, formal speech
Synonyms: discourse, declamation, sermon, address, homily

APPREHENSION (aa prih <u>hehn</u> shuhn) *n.*
suspicion or fear of future or unknown evil; the act of perceiving or comprehending; a legal seizure
Synonyms: concern, worry; understanding; capture

RESOLVE (rih <u>sahlv</u>) *v.* **-ing,-ed.**
1. to separate into distinct parts
Synonyms: disintegrate, break down
2. to determine or to make a firm decision about
Synonyms: solve, decide

DISPERSE (dihs <u>puhrs</u>) *v.* **-ing,-ed.**
to break up, scatter
Synonyms: dissipate, disintegrate, dispel

DRAW *v.* **-ing, drew, drawn.**
1. to lead to a certain assumption, to bring about on purpose
Synonyms: provoke, elicit
2. to pull, drag; to attract
Synonyms: haul, tow, lug; lure, entice

OBLIGING (uh <u>blie</u> jihng) *adj.*
able and ready to do favors, courteous
Synonyms: accomodating, compliant, yielding

funeral **oration** of one friend and client, and he could not help a certain **apprehension** lest the good name of another should be sucked down in the <u>eddy</u> of the scandal. It was, at least, a ticklish decision that he had to make, and, self-reliant as he was by habit, he began to cherish a longing for advice. It was not to be had directly; but perhaps, he thought, it might be fished for.

Presently after, he sat on one side of his own hearth, with Mr. Guest, his head clerk, upon the other, and midway between, at a nicely calculated distance from the fire, a bottle of a particular old wine that had long dwelt unsunned in the foundations of his house. The fog still slept on the wing above the drowned city, where the lamps glimmered like <u>carbuncles</u>, and through the muffle and smother of these fallen clouds, the procession of the town's life was still rolling in through the great arteries with a sound as of a mighty wind. But the room was gay with firelight. In the bottle the acids were long ago **resolved**. The <u>imperial dye</u> had softened with time, as the colour grows richer in stained windows, and the glow of hot autumn afternoons on hillside vineyards was ready to be set free and to **disperse** the fogs of London.

Insensibly the lawyer melted. There was no man from whom he kept fewer secrets than Mr. Guest, and he was not always sure that he kept as many as he meant. Guest had often been on business to the doctor's. He knew Poole. He could scarce have failed to hear of Mr. Hyde's familiarity about the house; he might **draw** conclusions. Was it not as well, then, that he should see a letter which put that mystery to rights, and above all—since Guest, being a great student and critic of handwriting—would consider the step natural and **obliging**? The clerk, besides, was a man of counsel; he would scarce read so strange a document without dropping a remark, and by that remark Mr. Utterson might shape his future course.

"This is a sad business about Sir Danvers," he said.

SAT VOCABULARY

ELICIT (ih <u>lih</u> siht) *v.* **-ing,-ed.**
  to draw out, provoke
    Synonyms: evoke, educe, wring, extract, tap

SEDULOUSLY (<u>seh</u> juh luhs lee) *adv.*
  with constant perseverance
    Synonyms: persistantly, carefully, attentively

SINGULAR (<u>sihn</u> gyuh luhr) *adj.*
  uncommon, peculiar
    Synonyms: unusual, odd, rare, unique, individual

REPOSE (rih <u>pohz</u>) *v.* **-ing,-ed.**
  1. to lie, to relax or rest
    Synonyms: sleep, slumber
  2. to be supported, to place (trust) or to count on
    Synonyms: depend, entrust, invest

"Yes, sir, indeed. It has **elicited** a great deal of public feeling," returned Guest. "The man, of course, was mad."

"I should like to hear your views on that," replied Utterson. "I have a document here in his handwriting. It is between ourselves, for I scarce know what to do about it; it is an ugly business at the best. But there it is, quite in your way: a murderer's autograph."

Guest's eyes brightened, and he sat down at once and studied it with passion. "No, sir," he said, "not mad. But it is an odd hand."

"And by all accounts a very odd writer," added the lawyer.

Just then the servant entered with a note.

"Is that from Dr. Jekyll, sir?" inquired the clerk. "I thought I knew the writing. Anything private, Mr. Utterson?"

"Only an invitation to dinner. Why? Do you want to see it?"

"One moment. I thank you, sir." The clerk laid the two sheets of paper alongside and **sedulously** compared their contents. "Thank you, sir," he said at last, returning both. "It's a very interesting autograph."

There was a pause, during which Mr. Utterson struggled with himself. "Why did you compare them, Guest?" he inquired suddenly.

"Well, sir," returned the clerk, "there's a rather **singular** resemblance. The two hands are in many points identical, only differently sloped."

"Rather quaint," said Utterson.

"It is, as you say, rather quaint," returned Guest.

"I wouldn't speak of this note, you know," said the master.

"No, sir," said the clerk. "I understand."

But no sooner was Mr. Utterson alone that night than he locked the note into his safe, where it **reposed** from that time forward. What! he thought. Henry Jekyll forge for a murderer! And his blood ran cold in his veins.

DISREPUTABLE (dihs <u>reh</u> pyuh tuh buhl) *adj.*
disgraceful, dishonorable, lacking respectability
Synonyms: infamous, shameful

CALLOUS (<u>kaa</u> luhs) *adj.*
insensitive, thick-skinned
Synonyms: impervious, indifferent, stony,
unmoved, unfeeling

VILE (viel) *adj.*
wretched, offensive, disgusting
Synonyms: despicable, nasty, depraved

DRAW *v.* **-ing, drew, drawn.**
1. to move steadily
Synonyms: proceed, continue, progress
2. to pull, drag; to attract
Synonyms: haul, tow, lug; lure, entice

SECLUSION (sih <u>cloo</u> zhuhn) *n.*
isolation, detachment
Synonyms: separation, privacy, solitude

REMARKABLE INCIDENT OF DR. LANYON

Time ran on. Thousands of pounds were offered in reward, for the death of Sir Danvers was resented as a public injury, but Mr. Hyde had disappeared out of the <u>ken</u> of the police as though he had never existed. Much of his past was unearthed, indeed, and all **disreputable**. Tales came out of the man's cruelty, at once so **callous** and violent, of his **vile** life, of his strange associates, of the hatred that seemed to have surrounded his career; but of his present whereabouts, not a whisper. From the time he had left the house in Soho on the morning of the murder, he was simply blotted out, and gradually, as time **drew** on, Mr. Utterson began to recover from the hotness of his alarm, and to grow more at quiet with himself. The death of Sir Danvers was, to his way of thinking, more than paid for by the disappearance of Mr. Hyde. Now that that evil influence had been withdrawn, a new life began for Dr. Jekyll. He came out of his **seclusion**, renewed relations with his friends, became once more their familiar guest and entertainer; and whilst he had always been known for charities, he was now no less distinguished for religion. He was busy, he was much in the open air, he did good. His face seemed to open and brighten, as if with an inward consciousness of service, and for more than two months the doctor was at peace.

On the 8th of January, Utterson had dined at the doctor's with a small party. Lanyon had been there, and the face of the host had looked from one to the other as in the old days when the trio were inseparable friends. On the 12th, and again on the 14th, the door was shut

SOLITUDE (<u>sahl</u> ih tood) *n.*
  time spent alone; social isolation
    Synonyms: loneliness; seclusion, withdrawal,
    retirement

LEGIBLY (<u>leh</u> juh blee) *adv.*
  in a readable way
    Synonyms: plainly, clearly

ALLUSION (uh <u>loo</u> zhuhn) *n.*
  indirect reference, an indication
    Synonyms: intimation, suggestion, hint

against the lawyer. "The doctor was confined to the house," Poole said, "and saw no one." On the 15th he tried again, and was again refused; and having now been used for the last two months to see his friend almost daily, he found this return of **solitude** to weigh upon his spirits. The fifth night he had in Guest to dine with him, and the sixth he betook himself to Dr. Lanyon's.

There at least he was not denied admittance, but when he came in, he was shocked at the change which had taken place in the doctor's appearance. He had his death-warrant written **legibly** upon his face. The rosy man had grown pale. His flesh had fallen away, he was visibly balder and older, and yet it was not so much these tokens of a swift physical decay that arrested the lawyer's notice as a look in the eye and quality of manner that seemed to testify to some deep-seated terror of the mind. It was unlikely that the doctor should fear death, and yet that was what Utterson was tempted to suspect. Yes, he thought, he is a doctor, he must know his own state and that his days are counted; and the knowledge is more than he can bear. And yet when Utterson remarked on his ill looks, it was with an air of great firmness that Lanyon declared himself a doomed man.

"I have had a shock," he said, "and I shall never recover. It is a question of weeks. Well, life has been pleasant. I liked it, yes, sir, I used to like it. I sometimes think if we knew all, we should be more glad to get away."

"Jekyll is ill, too," observed Utterson. "Have you seen him?"

But Lanyon's face changed, and he held up a trembling hand. "I wish to see or hear no more of Dr. Jekyll," he said in a loud, unsteady voice. "I am quite done with that person, and I beg that you will spare me any **allusion** to one whom I regard as dead."

PATHETICALLY (puh <u>theh</u> tihk lee) *adv.*
in a manner capable of arousing pity or compassion
Synonyms: miserably, woefully, hopelessly

INCURABLE (ihn <u>kyuhr</u> uh buhl) *adj.*
not able to be cured or fixed
Synonyms: hopeless, irrecoverable, irreparable

SECLUSION (sih <u>cloo</u> zhuhn) *n.*
isolation, detachment
Synonyms: separation, privacy, solitude

"Tut, tut," said Mr. Utterson, and then, after a considerable pause, "can't I do anything? We are three very old friends, Lanyon. We shall not live to make others."

"Nothing can be done," returned Lanyon. "Ask himself."

"He will not see me," said the lawyer.

"I am not surprised at that," was the reply. "Some day, Utterson, after I am dead, you may perhaps come to learn the right and wrong of this. I cannot tell you. And in the meantime, if you can sit and talk with me of other things, for God's sake, stay and do so. But if you cannot keep clear of this accursed topic, then, in God's name, go, for I cannot bear it."

As soon as he got home, Utterson sat down and wrote to Jekyll, complaining of his exclusion from the house and asking the cause of this unhappy break with Lanyon, and the next day brought him a long answer, often very **pathetically** worded and sometimes darkly mysterious in drift. The quarrel with Lanyon was **incurable**. "I do not blame our old friend," Jekyll wrote, "but I share his view that we must never meet. I mean from henceforth to lead a life of extreme **seclusion**. You must not be surprised, nor must you doubt my friendship, if my door is often shut even to you. You must suffer me to go my own dark way. I have brought on myself a punishment and a danger that I cannot name. If I am the chief of sinners, I am the chief of sufferers also. I could not think that this earth contained a place for sufferings and terrors so <u>unmanning</u>, and you can do but one thing, Utterson, to lighten this destiny, and that is to respect my silence."

Utterson was amazed. The dark influence of Hyde had been withdrawn, the doctor had returned to his old tasks and <u>amities</u>—a week ago, the prospect had smiled with every promise of a cheerful and an honoured age, and now in a moment, friendship and peace of mind

MELANCHOLY (mehl uhn <u>kahl</u> ee) *adj.*
  sad, depressing
    Synonyms: dejected, despondent, woeful,
    sorrowful

DRAW *v.* **-ing, drew, drawn.**
  to pull, drag; to attract
    Synonyms: haul, tow, lug; lure, entice

EMPHATICALLY (ehm <u>faa</u> tihk lee) *adv.*
  with extra force or energy, with extra emphasis
    Synonyms: insistently, definitely, strikingly

STRINGENT (<u>strihn</u> juhnt) *adj.*
  imposing severe, rigorous standards
    Synonyms: restricted, tight, demanding

OBLIGATION (ah blih <u>gay</u> shuhn) *n.*
  a sense of duty or promise; a requirement or force to
  obey
    Synonyms: responsibility; constraint, bind,
    committment

MORTIFY (<u>mohr</u> tih fie) *v.* **-ing,-ied.**
  1. to control or deny one's own needs and desires
    Synonyms: dismiss, shun, disregard
  2. to humiliate or make someone feel shame
    Synonyms: embarrass, humble, abase

and the whole tenor of his life were wrecked. So great and unprepared a change pointed to madness, but in view of Lanyon's manner and words, there must lie for it some deeper ground.

A week afterwards Dr. Lanyon took to his bed, and in something less than a <u>fortnight</u> he was dead. The night after the funeral, at which he had been sadly affected, Utterson locked the door of his business room and, sitting there by the light of a **melancholy** candle, **drew** out and set before him an envelope addressed by the hand and sealed with the seal of his dead friend. "PRIVATE: for the hands of J. G. Utterson ALONE, and in case of his predecease *to be destroyed unread*," so it was **emphatically** <u>superscribed</u>, and the lawyer dreaded to behold the contents. I have buried one friend today, he thought. What if this should cost me another? And then he condemned the fear as a disloyalty, and broke the seal.

Within there was another enclosure, likewise sealed, and marked upon the cover as "not to be opened till the death or disappearance of Dr. Henry Jekyll." Utterson could not trust his eyes. Yes, it was disappearance. Here again, as in the mad will, which he had long ago restored to its author, here again were the idea of a disappearance and the name of Henry Jekyll bracketed. But in the will, that idea had sprung from the sinister suggestion of the man Hyde. It was set there with a purpose all too plain and horrible. Written by the hand of Lanyon, what should it mean? A great curiosity came to the trustee, to disregard the <u>prohibition</u> and dive at once to the bottom of these mysteries. But professional honour and faith to his dead friend were **stringent obligations**, and the packet slept in the inmost corner of his private safe.

It is one thing to **mortify** curiosity, another to conquer it, and it may be doubted if, from that day forth,

SAT VOCABULARY

DISQUIET (dihs <u>kwie</u> uht) *v.* **-ing,-ed.**
to take away the peace or tranquility of, to unsettle
Synonyms: worry, agitate, distress, disturb

INSCRUTABLE (ihn <u>skroo</u> tuh buhl) *adj.*
impossible to understand fully
Synonyms: mysterious, impenetrable, cryptic, enigmatic

RECLUSE (<u>rehk</u> kloos) (rih <u>kloos</u>) *n.*
a person who is shut off from the world
Synonyms: solitaire, hermit

Utterson desired the society of his surviving friend with the same eagerness. He thought of him kindly, but his thoughts were **disquieted** and fearful. He went to call indeed, but he was perhaps relieved to be denied admittance. Perhaps, in his heart, he preferred to speak with Poole upon the doorstep, and surrounded by the air and sounds of the open city, rather than to be admitted into that house of voluntary bondage, and to sit and speak with its **inscrutable recluse**. Poole had, indeed, no very pleasant news to communicate. The doctor, it appeared, now more than ever confined himself to the cabinet over the laboratory, where he would sometimes even sleep. He was out of spirits, he had grown very silent, he did not read; it seemed as if he had something on his mind. Utterson became so used to the unvarying character of these reports, that he fell off little by little in the frequency of his visits.

REPULSION (rih <u>puhl</u> shuhn) *n.*
   hatred, disgust
      Synonyms: aversion, abhorrence

MIEN (meen) *n.*
   characteristics expressive of attitude or personality
      Synonyms: manner, demeanor, expression, style

DISCONSOLATE (dihs <u>kahn</u> soh liht) *adj.*
   hopelessly sad, forlorn
      Synonyms: dismal, inconsolable, comfortless

INCIDENT AT THE WINDOW

It chanced on Sunday, when Mr. Utterson was on his usual walk with Mr. Enfield, that their way lay once again through the by-street, and that when they came in front of the door, both stopped to gaze on it.

"Well," said Enfield, "that story's at an end, at least. We shall never see more of Mr. Hyde."

"I hope not," said Utterson. "Did I ever tell you that I once saw him, and shared your feeling of **repulsion**?"

"It was impossible to do the one without the other," returned Enfield. "And, by the way, what an ass you must have thought me, not to know that this was a back way to Dr. Jekyll's! It was partly your own fault that I found it out, even when I did."

"So you found it out, did you?" said Utterson. "But if that be so, we may step into the court and take a look at the windows. To tell you the truth, I am uneasy about poor Jekyll, and even outside, I feel as if the presence of a friend might do him good."

The court was very cool and a little damp, and full of premature twilight, although the sky, high up overhead, was still bright with sunset. The middle one of the three windows was halfway open, and sitting close beside it, taking the air with an infinite sadness of **mien**, like some **disconsolate** prisoner, Utterson saw Dr. Jekyll.

"What! Jekyll!" he cried. "I trust you are better."

"I am very low, Utterson," replied the doctor drearily, "very low. It will not last long, thank God."

"You stay too much indoors," said the lawyer. "You should be out, whipping up the circulation like Mr. Enfield and me. (This is my cousin—Mr. Enfield—Dr.

ABJECT (<u>aab</u> jehkt) *adj.*
  miserable, pitiful
    Synonyms: pathetic, lamentable, sorry

TRAVERSE (truh <u>vuhrs</u>) (traa <u>vuhrs</u>) *v.* **-ing,-ed.**
  to travel or move across; to turn or move laterally
    Synonyms: cross, intersect, pass through; swivel,
    zigzag

Jekyll.) Come now; get your hat and take a quick turn with us."

"You are very good," sighed the other. "I should like to very much, but no, no, no, it is quite impossible; I dare not. But indeed, Utterson, I am very glad to see you; this is really a great pleasure. I would ask you and Mr. Enfield up, but the place is really not fit."

"Why then," said the lawyer good-naturedly, "the best thing we can do is to stay down here and speak with you from where we are."

"That is just what I was about to venture to propose," returned the doctor, with a smile. But the words were hardly uttered before the smile was struck out of his face and succeeded by an expression of such **abject** terror and despair as froze the very blood of the two gentlemen below. They saw it but for a glimpse, for the window was instantly thrust down but that glimpse had been sufficient, and they turned and left the court without a word. In silence, too, they **traversed** the by-street; and it was not until they had come into a neighbouring thoroughfare, where even upon a Sunday there were still some stirrings of life, that Mr. Utterson at last turned and looked at his companion. They were both pale, and there was an answering horror in their eyes.

"God forgive us! God forgive us!" said Mr. Utterson.

But Mr. Enfield only nodded his head very seriously and walked on once more in silence.

EXPLICIT (ehk <u>splih</u> siht) *adj.*
clearly defined, specific, forthright in expression
Synonyms: express, categorical, definite,
unequivocal

DOGGEDLY (<u>daw</u> guhd lee) *adv.*
stubbornly or persistently
Synonyms: tenaciously, obstinately, pertinaciously

AMPLY (<u>aam</u> plee) *adv.*
to a large or great degree
Synonyms: sufficiently, fully, generously

AMISS (uh <u>mihs</u>) *adj.*
out of place
Synonyms: astray, awry, lost, wrong

THE LAST NIGHT

Mr. Utterson was sitting by his fireside one evening after dinner when he was surprised to receive a visit from Poole.

"Bless me, Poole, what brings you here?" he cried. And then, taking a second look at him, "What ails you?" he added. "Is the doctor ill?"

"Mr. Utterson," said the man, "there is something wrong."

"Take a seat, and here is a glass of wine for you," said the lawyer. "Now, take your time and tell me plainly what you want."

"You know the doctor's ways, sir," replied Poole, "and how he shuts himself up. Well, he's shut up again in the cabinet, and I don't like it, sir—I wish I may die if I like it. Mr. Utterson, sir, I'm afraid."

"Now, my good man," said the lawyer, "be **explicit**. What are you afraid of?"

"I've been afraid for about a week," returned Poole, **doggedly** disregarding the question, "and I can bear it no more."

The man's appearance **amply** bore out his words. His manner was altered for the worse; and except for the moment when he had first announced his terror, he had not once looked the lawyer in the face. Even now, he sat with the glass of wine untasted on his knee and his eyes directed to a corner of the floor. "I can bear it no more," he repeated.

"Come," said the lawyer, "I see you have some good reason, Poole; I see there is something seriously **amiss**. Try to tell me what it is."

INCLINE (ihn <u>klien</u>) *v.* **-ing,-ed.**
1. to have a specific tendency, to be predisposed
   Synonyms: lean to, influence, impel, prefer
2. to bend or tilt upward
   Synonyms: slope, slant, lean, deviate, point

DIAPHANOUS (die <u>aaf</u> uh nuhs) *adj.*
allowing light to show through; delicate
   Synonyms: sheer, transparent, gauzy, translucent;
   tenuous, flimsy, fragile, dainty

CALAMITY (kuh <u>laam</u> ih tee) *n.*
misfortune; state of despair
   Synonyms: disaster, cataclysm; misery

"I think there's been foul play," said Poole, hoarsely.

"Foul play!" cried the lawyer, a good deal frightened and rather **inclined** to be irritated in consequence. "What foul play? What does the man mean?"

"I daren't say, sir," was the answer, "but will you come along with me and see for yourself?"

Mr. Utterson's only answer was to rise and get his hat and greatcoat. But he observed with wonder the greatness of the relief that appeared upon the butler's face, and perhaps with no less, that the wine was still untasted when he set it down to follow.

It was a wild, cold, seasonable night of March, with a pale moon, lying on her back as though the wind had tilted her, and a flying <u>wrack</u> of the most **diaphanous** and <u>lawny</u> texture. The wind made talking difficult, and flecked the blood into the face. It seemed to have swept the streets unusually bare of passengers, besides, for Mr. Utterson thought he had never seen that part of London so deserted. He could have wished it otherwise. Never in his life had he been conscious of so sharp a wish to see and touch his fellow-creatures, for struggle as he might, there was borne in upon his mind a crushing anticipation of **calamity**. The square, when they got there, was all full of wind and dust, and the thin trees in the garden were lashing themselves along the railing. Poole, who had kept all the way a pace or two ahead, now pulled up in the middle of the pavement, and in spite of the biting weather, took off his hat and mopped his brow with a red pocket-handkerchief. But for all the hurry of his coming, these were not the dews of exertion that he wiped away, but the moisture of some strangling anguish, for his face was white, and his voice, when he spoke, harsh and broken.

"Well, sir," he said, "here we are, and God grant there be nothing wrong."

"Amen, Poole," said the lawyer.

FEROCITY (fuhr <u>ah</u> sih tee) *n.*
fierceness, violence
  Synonyms: fury, wildness, vehemence, turbulence

LAMENTATION (laa mehn <u>tay</u> shuhn) *n.*
an expression of grief or sorrow, a loud cry
  Synonyms: complaint, moaning, sobbing, tears

TERMINATION (tuhr mih <u>nay</u> shuhn) *n.*
the act of ending or setting bounds; an end, outcome
or result
  Synonyms: limitation, conclusion; close, finish

Thereupon the servant knocked in a very guarded manner. The door was opened on the chain, and a voice asked from within, "Is that you, Poole?"

"It's all right," said Poole. "Open the door."

The hall, when they entered it, was brightly lighted up. The fire was built high, and about the hearth the whole of the servants, men and women, stood huddled together like a flock of sheep. At the sight of Mr. Utterson, the housemaid broke into hysterical whimpering, and the cook, crying out, "Bless God! It's Mr. Utterson," ran forward as if to take him in her arms.

"What, what? Are you all here?" said the lawyer, peevishly. "Very irregular, very unseemly. Your master would be far from pleased."

"They're all afraid," said Poole.

Blank silence followed, no one protesting; only the maid lifted up her voice and now wept loudly.

"Hold your tongue!" Poole said to her, with a **ferocity** of accent that testified to his own jangled nerves. And indeed, when the girl had so suddenly raised the note of her **lamentation**, they had all started and turned towards the inner door with faces of dreadful expectation. "And now," continued the butler, addressing the knife-boy, "reach me a candle, and we'll get this through hands at once." And then he begged Mr. Utterson to follow him, and led the way to the back garden.

"Now, sir," said he, "you come as gently as you can. I want you to hear, and I don't want you to be heard. And see here, sir, if by any chance he was to ask you in, don't go."

Mr. Utterson's nerves, at this unlooked-for **termination**, gave a jerk that nearly threw him from his balance, but he re-collected his courage, and followed the butler into the laboratory building and through the surgical theatre, with its lumber of crates and bottles, to the foot of the stair. Here Poole motioned him to stand

RESOLUTION (reh suh <u>loo</u> shuhn) *n.*
  a firm decision
      Synonyms: determination, will, explanation

INDUCE (ih <u>doos</u>) (ihn <u>dyoos</u>) *v.* **-ing,-ed.**
  to persuade; bring about
      Synonyms: convince, prevail; effect, lead, occasion

COMMEND (kuh <u>mehnd</u>) *v.* **-ing,-ed.**
  to represent as worthy; to entrust or hand over in
  care; to praise or show respect
      Synonyms: qualify, deserve; assign, relegate;
      flatter, compliment

on one side and listen, while he himself, setting down the candle and making a great and obvious call on his **resolution**, mounted the steps, and knocked with a somewhat uncertain hand on the red <u>baize</u> of the cabinet door.

"Mr. Utterson, sir, asking to see you," he called, and even as he did so, once more violently signed to the lawyer to give ear.

A voice answered from within. "Tell him I cannot see anyone," it said complainingly.

"Thank you, sir," said Poole, with a note of something like triumph in his voice, and taking up his candle, he led Mr. Utterson back across the yard and into the great kitchen, where the fire was out and the beetles were leaping on the floor.

"Sir," he said, looking Mr. Utterson in the eyes, "was that my master's voice?"

"It seems much changed," replied the lawyer, very pale, but giving look for look.

"Changed? Well, yes, I think so," said the butler. "Have I been twenty years in this man's house, to be deceived about his voice? No, sir, master's made away with. He was made away with eight days ago, when we heard him cry out upon the name of God, and *who's* in there instead of him, and *why* it stays there, is a thing that cries to Heaven, Mr. Utterson!"

"This is a very strange tale, Poole. This is rather a wild tale, my man," said Mr. Utterson, biting his finger. "Suppose it were as you suppose, supposing Dr. Jekyll to have been—well, murdered, what could **induce** the murderer to stay? That won't hold water, it doesn't **commend** itself to reason."

"Well, Mr. Utterson, you are a hard man to satisfy, but I'll do it yet," said Poole. "All this last week (you must know) him, or it, or whatever it is that lives in that cabinet, has been crying night and day for some sort of

SEDULOUS (<u>seh</u> juh luhs) *adj.*
   constant and persevering
      Synonyms: persistant, careful, attentive

medicine and cannot get it to his mind. It was sometimes his way—the master's, that is—to write his orders
on a sheet of paper and throw it on the stair. We've had
nothing else this week back; nothing but papers and a
closed door and the very meals left there to be smuggled
in when nobody was looking. Well, sir, every day, ay,
and twice and thrice in the same day, there have been
orders and complaints, and I have been sent flying to all
the wholesale chemists in town. Every time I brought
the stuff back, there would be another paper telling me
to return it, because it was not pure, and another order
to a different firm. This drug is wanted bitter bad, sir,
whatever for."

"Have you any of these papers?" asked Mr. Utterson.

Poole felt in his pocket and handed out a crumpled
note, which the lawyer, bending nearer to the candle,
carefully examined. Its contents ran thus: "Dr. Jekyll
presents his compliments to Messrs. Maw. He assures
them that their last sample is impure and quite useless
for his present purpose. In the year 18——, Dr. J. pur-
chased a somewhat large quantity from Messrs. M. He
now begs them to search with the most **sedulous** care,
and should any of the same quality be left, to forward it
to him at once. Expense is no consideration. The importance of this to Dr. J. can hardly be exaggerated." So far
the letter had run composedly enough, but here, with a
sudden splutter of the pen, the writer's emotion had
broken loose. "For God's sake," he had added, "find me
some of the old."

"This is a strange note," said Mr. Utterson. And then
sharply, "How do you come to have it open?"

"The man at Maw's was main angry, sir, and he threw
it back to me like so much dirt," returned Poole.

"This is unquestionably the doctor's hand, do you
know?" resumed the lawyer.

"I thought it looked like it," said the servant rather

MALADY (<u>maal</u> uh dee) *n.*
  illness
    Synonyms: disease, disorder, ailment, affliction,
    infirmity

DEFORM (dih <u>fohrm</u>) *v.* **-ing,-ed.**
  to disfigure, spoil
    Synonyms: contort, twist, mar, misshape

RETAIN (rih <u>tayn</u>) *v.* **-ing,-ed.**
  to hold, keep possession of
    Synonyms: withhold, reserve, maintain, remember

APPALLING (uh <u>pahl</u> lihng) *adj.*
  shocking, dismaying
    Synonyms: horrifying, dreadful, astounding

EXORBITANT (ihg <u>zor</u> bih tuhnt) *adj.*
  greater than reasonable, extravagant
    Synonyms: excessive, immoderate, inordinate

PALLOR (<u>paal</u> uhr) *n.*
  extreme paleness of the skin
    Synonyms: lividity, wanness

sulkily. And then, with another voice, "But what matters hand of write?" he said. "I've seen him!"

"Seen him?" repeated Mr. Utterson. "Well?"

"That's it!" said Poole. "It was this way. I came suddenly into the theatre from the garden. It seems he had slipped out to look for this drug, or whatever it is, for the cabinet door was open, and there he was at the far end of the room digging among the crates. He looked up when I came in, gave a kind of cry, and whipped upstairs into the cabinet. It was but for one minute that I saw him, but the hair stood upon my head like quills. Sir, if that was my master, why had he a mask upon his face? If it was my master, why did he cry out like a rat and run from me? I have served him long enough. And then . . ." The man paused and passed his hand over his face.

"These are all very strange circumstances," said Mr. Utterson, "but I think I begin to see daylight. Your master, Poole, is plainly seized with one of those **maladies** that both torture and **deform** the sufferer. Hence, for <u>aught</u> I know, the alteration of his voice; hence the mask and his avoidance of his friends; hence his eagerness to find this drug, by means of which the poor soul **retains** some hope of ultimate recovery—God grant that he be not deceived! There is my explanation. It is sad enough, Poole, ay, and **appalling** to consider, but it is plain and natural, hangs well together, and delivers us from all **exorbitant** alarms."

"Sir," said the butler, turning to a sort of mottled **pallor**, "that thing was not my master, and there's the truth. My master"—here he looked round him and began to whisper—"is a tall fine build of a man, and this was more of a dwarf." Utterson attempted to protest. "Oh, sir," cried Poole, "do you think I do not know my master after twenty years? Do you think I do not know where his head comes to in the cabinet door,

UNDAUNTED (uhn <u>dawn</u> tihd) *adj.*
  bold, valiant, not discouraged or intimidated
    Synonyms: brave, courageous, fearless, intrepid

PERIL (<u>pehr</u> ihl) *n.*
  danger
    Synonyms: trouble, hazard, risk

where I saw him every morning of my life? No, sir, that thing in the mask was never Dr. Jekyll—God knows what it was, but it was never Dr. Jekyll. And it is the belief of my heart that there was murder done."

"Poole," replied the lawyer, "if you say that, it will become my duty to make certain. Much as I desire to spare your master's feelings, much as I am puzzled about this note, which seems to prove him to be still alive, I shall consider it my duty to break in that door."

"Ah, Mr. Utterson, that's talking!" cried the butler.

"And now comes the second question," resumed Utterson. "Who is going to do it?"

"Why, you and me, sir," was the **undaunted** reply.

"That is very well said," returned the lawyer, "and whatever comes of it, I shall make it my business to see you are no loser."

"There is an axe in the theatre," continued Poole, "and you might take the kitchen poker for yourself."

The lawyer took that rude but weighty instrument into his hand and balanced it. "Do you know, Poole," he said, looking up, "that you and I are about to place ourselves in a position of some **peril**?"

"You may say so, sir, indeed," returned the butler.

"It is well, then, that we should be frank," said the other. "We both think more than we have said. Let us make a clean breast. This masked figure that you saw, did you recognise it?"

"Well, sir, it went so quick, and the creature was so doubled up, that I could hardly swear to that," was the answer. "But if you mean, was it Mr. Hyde? Why, yes, I think it was! You see, it was much of the same bigness, and it had the same quick light way with it. And then who else could have got in by the laboratory door? You have not forgot, sir, that at the time of the murder he had still the key with him? But that's not all. I don't know, Mr. Utterson, if ever you met this Mr. Hyde?"

INCLINE (ihn <u>klien</u>) *v.* **-ing,-ed.**
1. to have a specific tendency, to be predisposed
   Synonyms: lean to, influence, impel, prefer
2. to bend or tilt upward
   Synonyms: slope, slant, lean, deviate, point

LURK (luhrk) *v.* **-ing,-ed.**
to hide, to lie hidden or unsuspected; to prowl, sneak
   Synonyms: conceal; stalk, creep, skulk, slink

VENGEANCE (<u>vehn</u> juhns) *n.*
punishment inflicted in retaliation; vehemence
   Synonyms: revenge, repayment; wrath

SUSPENSE (suh <u>spents</u>) *n.*
a feeling of anxiety caused by a mysterious situation
   Synonyms: apprehension, anticipation, waiting

AMISS (uh <u>mihs</u>) *adj.*
out of place
   Synonyms: astray, awry, lost, wrong

MALEFACTOR (<u>maal</u> uh faak tuhr) *n.*
evil-doer, culprit
   Synonyms: criminal, offender, felon

"Yes," said the lawyer, "I once spoke with him."

"Then you must know, as well as the rest of us, that there was something queer about that gentleman—something that gave a man a turn. I don't know rightly how to say it, sir, beyond this: that you felt in your marrow—kind of cold and thin."

"I own I felt something of what you describe," said Mr. Utterson.

"Quite so, sir," returned Poole. "Well, when that masked thing like a monkey jumped up from among the chemicals and whipped into the cabinet, it went down my spine like ice. Oh, I know it's not evidence, Mr. Utterson—I'm book-learned enough for that—but a man has his feelings, and I give you my bible-word it was Mr. Hyde!"

"Ay, ay," said the lawyer. "My fears **incline** to the same point. Evil, I fear, founded—evil was sure to come—of that connection. Ay, truly, I believe you, I believe poor Harry is killed, and I believe his murderer (for what purpose, God alone can tell) is still **lurking** in his victim's room. Well, let our name be **vengeance**. Call Bradshaw."

The footman came at the summons, very white and nervous.

"Pull yourself together, Bradshaw," said the lawyer. "This **suspense**, I know, is telling upon all of you, but it is now our intention to make an end of it. Poole, here, and I are going to force our way into the cabinet. If all is well, my shoulders are broad enough to bear the blame. Meanwhile, lest anything should really be **amiss**, or any **malefactor** seek to escape by the back, you and the boy must go round the corner with a pair of good sticks and take your post at the laboratory door. We give you ten minutes to get to your stations."

As Bradshaw left, the lawyer looked at his watch. "And now, Poole, let us get to ours," he said, and taking

SOLEMNLY (<u>sah</u> luhm lee) *adv.*
  seriously or somberly
    Synonyms: quietly, earnestly, ceremonially

DRAW *v.* **-ing, drew, drawn.**
  1. to move steadily
    Synonyms: proceed, continue, progress
  2. to pull, drag; to attract
    Synonyms: haul, tow, lug; lure, entice

DISINTER (dihs ihn <u>tuhr</u>) *v.* **-ring,-red.**
  to bring out into the open; to dig up from a grave
    Synonyms: disclose, reveal; exhume

BATED (<u>bay</u> tihd) *adj.*
  lessened or restrained, often used to describe one's
  breath during a time of great anticipation
    Synonyms: lowered, reduced, diminished

the poker under his arm, he led the way into the yard. The scud had banked over the moon, and it was now quite dark. The wind, which only broke in puffs and <u>draughts</u> into that deep well of building, tossed the light of the candle to and fro about their steps, until they came into the shelter of the theatre, where they sat down silently to wait. London hummed **solemnly** all around; but nearer at hand, the stillness was only broken by the sound of a footfall moving to and fro along the cabinet floor.

"So it will walk all day, sir," whispered Poole. "Ay, and the better part of the night. Only when a new sample comes from the chemist, there's a bit of a break. Ah, it's an ill conscience that's such an enemy to rest! Ah, sir, there's blood foully shed in every step of it! But hark again, a little closer—put your heart in your ears, Mr. Utterson, and tell me, is that the doctor's foot?"

The steps fell lightly and oddly, with a certain swing, for all they went so slowly. It was different indeed from the heavy creaking tread of Henry Jekyll. Utterson sighed. "Is there never anything else?" he asked.

Poole nodded. "Once," he said. "Once I heard it weeping!"

"Weeping? How that?" said the lawyer, conscious of a sudden chill of horror.

"Weeping like a woman or a lost soul," said the butler. "I came away with that upon my heart, that I could have wept too."

But now the ten minutes **drew** to an end. Poole **disinterred** the axe from under a stack of packing straw, the candle was set upon the nearest table to light them to the attack, and they **drew** near with **bated** breath to where that patient foot was still going up and down, up and down in the quiet of the night.

"Jekyll," cried Utterson with a loud voice, "I demand to see you." He paused a moment, but there came no

BESIEGER (bih <u>seej</u> uhr) *n.*
person who attacks or surrounds with armed forces
Synonyms: enemy, invader, assailant

APPALL (uh <u>pahl</u>) *v.* **-ing,-ed.**
to overcome or be overcome with shock or dismay
Synonyms: horrify, astound, petrify

DRAW *v.* **-ing, drew, drawn.**
1. to move steadily
Synonyms: proceed, continue, progress
2. to pull, drag; to attract
Synonyms: haul, tow, lug; lure, entice

reply. "I give you fair warning. Our suspicions are aroused, and I must and shall see you," he resumed, "if not by fair means, then by foul—if not of your consent, then by brute force!"

"Utterson," said the voice, "for God's sake, have mercy!"

"Ah, that's not Jekyll's voice—it's Hyde's!" cried Utterson. "Down with the door, Poole!"

Poole swung the axe over his shoulder; the blow shook the building, and the red <u>baize</u> door leaped against the lock and hinges. A dismal screech, as of mere animal terror, rang from the cabinet. Up went the axe again, and again the panels crashed and the frame bounded. Four times the blow fell; but the wood was tough and the fittings were of excellent workmanship. It was not until the fifth that the lock burst in sunder, and the wreck of the door fell inwards on the carpet.

The **besiegers**, **appalled** by their own riot and the stillness that had succeeded, stood back a little and peered in. There lay the cabinet before their eyes in the quiet lamplight, a good fire glowing and chattering on the hearth, the kettle singing its thin strain, a drawer or two open, papers neatly set forth on the business table, and nearer the fire, the things laid out for tea. The quietest room, you would have said, and, but for the glazed presses full of chemicals, the most commonplace that night in London.

Right in the midst there lay the body of a man sorely contorted and still twitching. They **drew** near on tiptoe, turned it on its back, and beheld the face of Edward Hyde. He was dressed in clothes far too large for him, clothes of the doctor's bigness. The <u>cords</u> of his face still moved with a semblance of life, but life was quite gone, and by the crushed <u>phial</u> in the hand and the strong

smell of kernels that hung upon the air, Utterson knew that he was looking on the body of a self-destroyer.

"We have come too late," he said sternly, "whether to save or punish. Hyde is gone to his account, and it only remains for us to find the body of your master."

The far greater proportion of the building was occupied by the theatre, which filled almost the whole ground storey and was lighted from above, and by the cabinet, which formed an upper storey at one end and looked upon the court. A corridor joined the theatre to the door on the by-street, and with this, the cabinet communicated separately by a second flight of stairs. There were besides a few dark closets and a spacious cellar. All these they now thoroughly examined. Each closet needed but a glance, for all were empty, and all, by the dust that fell from their doors, had stood long unopened. The cellar, indeed, was filled with crazy lumber, mostly dating from the times of the surgeon who was Jekyll's predecessor. But even as they opened the door, they were advertised of the uselessness of further search by the fall of a perfect mat of cobweb which had for years sealed up the entrance. Nowhere was there any trace of Henry Jekyll, dead or alive.

Poole stamped on the flags of the corridor. "He must be buried here," he said, hearkening to the sound.

"Or he may have fled," said Utterson, and he turned to examine the door in the by-street. It was locked, and lying near by on the flags, they found the key, already stained with rust.

"This does not look like use," observed the lawyer.

"Use!" echoed Poole. "Do you not see, sir, it is broken? Much as if a man had stamped on it."

"Ah," continued Utterson, "and the fractures, too, are rusty." The two men looked at each other with a scare. "This is beyond me, Poole," said the lawyer. "Let us go back to the cabinet."

DRAW *v.* **-ing, drew, drawn.**
   to pull, drag; to attract
      Synonyms: haul, tow, lug; lure, entice

PIOUS (<u>pie</u> uhs) *adj.*
   dedicated, devout, extremely religious
      Synonyms: observant, reverent, sanctimonious

BLASPHEMY (<u>blaas</u> fuh mee) *n.*
   an act of profanity, an act of reviling something
   sacred
      Synonyms: curse, indignity, impiety, abuse, sacrilege

COUNTENANCE (<u>kown</u> tuh nuhns) *n.*
   appearance, facial expression
      Synonyms: face, features, visage

They mounted the stair in silence, and still, with an occasional awestruck glance at the dead body, proceeded more thoroughly to examine the contents of the cabinet. At one table, there were traces of chemical work, various measured heaps of some white salt being laid on glass saucers, as though for an experiment in which the unhappy man had been prevented.

"That is the same drug that I was always bringing him," said Poole; and even as he spoke, the kettle with a startling noise boiled over.

This brought them to the fireside, where the easy chair was **drawn** cosily up, and the tea things stood ready to the sitter's elbow, the very sugar in the cup. There were several books on a shelf. One lay beside the tea things open, and Utterson was amazed to find it a copy of a **pious** work for which Jekyll had several times expressed a great esteem, annotated, in his own hand, with startling **blasphemies**.

Next, in the course of their review of the chamber, the searchers came to the <u>cheval-glass</u>, into whose depth they looked with an involuntary horror. But it was so turned as to show them nothing but the rosy glow playing on the roof, the fire sparkling in a hundred repetitions along the glazed front of the presses, and their own pale and fearful **countenances** stooping to look in.

"This glass has seen some strange things, sir," whispered Poole.

"And surely none stranger than itself," echoed the lawyer, in the same tone. "For what did Jekyll"—he caught himself up at the word with a start, and then conquering the weakness—"what could Jekyll want with it?" he said.

"You may say that!" said Poole.

Next they turned to the business table. On the desk, among the neat array of papers, a large envelope was

MALEFACTOR (<u>maal</u> uh faak tuhr) *n.*
  evil-doer, culprit
    Synonyms: criminal, offender, felon

DISPOSE (dih <u>spohz</u>) *v.* **-ing,-ed.**
  1. to get rid of
    Synonyms: discard, throw out
  2. to put in place, to settle; to incline or give a
  tendency to
    Synonyms: organize, position; determine, motivate

SOLEMNLY (<u>sah</u> luhm lee) *adv.*
  seriously or somberly
    Synonyms: quietly, earnestly, ceremonially

uppermost and bore, in the doctor's hand, the name of Mr. Utterson. The lawyer unsealed it, and several enclosures fell to the floor. The first was a will, drawn in the same eccentric terms as the one which he had returned six months before, to serve as a testament in case of death and as a deed of gift in case of disappearance. But in place of the name of Edward Hyde, the lawyer, with indescribable amazement, read the name of Gabriel John Utterson. He looked at Poole, and then back at the papers, and last of all at the dead **malefactor** stretched upon the carpet.

"My head goes round," he said. "He has been all these days in possession. He had no cause to like me, he must have raged to see himself displaced, and he has not destroyed this document."

He caught the next paper; it was a brief note in the doctor's hand and dated at the top. "Oh, Poole!" the lawyer cried, "he was alive and here this day. He cannot have been **disposed** of in so short a space; he must be still alive, he must have fled! And then, why fled? And how? And in that case, can we venture to declare this suicide? Oh, we must be careful. I foresee that we may yet involve your master in some dire catastrophe."

"Why don't you read it, sir?" asked Poole.

"Because I fear," replied the lawyer, **solemnly**. "God grant I have no cause for it!" And with that he brought the paper to his eyes, and read as follows:

My dear Utterson—When this shall fall into your hands, I shall have disappeared, under what circumstances I have not the penetration to foresee, but my instinct and all the circumstances of my nameless situation tell me that the end is sure and must be early. Go then, and first read the narrative which Lanyon warned me he was to place in your hands.

And if you care to hear more, turn to the confession of

> Your unworthy and unhappy friend,
> Henry Jekyll

"There was a third enclosure?" asked Utterson.

"Here, sir," said Poole, and gave into his hands a considerable packet sealed in several places.

The lawyer put it in his pocket. "I would say nothing of this paper. If your master has fled or is dead, we may at least save his credit. It is now ten. I must go home and read these documents in quiet, but I shall be back before midnight, when we shall send for the police."

They went out, locking the door of the theatre behind them, and Utterson, once more leaving the servants gathered about the fire in the hall, trudged back to his office to read the two narratives in which this mystery was now to be explained.

PREFACE (<u>preh</u> fuhs) *n.*
  introduction to a book; introductory remarks to a
  speech
    Synonyms: foreword, preamble, prelude, prologue

Dr. Lanyon's Narrative

On the ninth of January, now four days ago, I received by the evening delivery a registered envelope, addressed in the hand of my colleague and old school companion, Henry Jekyll. I was a good deal surprised by this, for we were by no means in the habit of correspondence. I had seen the man, dined with him, indeed, the night before and I could imagine nothing in our intercourse that should justify the formality of registration. The contents increased my wonder; for this is how the letter ran:

10th December 18——

Dear Lanyon—You are one of my oldest friends, and although we may have differed at times on scientific questions, I cannot remember, at least on my side, any break in our affection. There was never a day when, if you had said to me, "Jekyll, my life, my honour, my reason, depend upon you," I would not have sacrificed my fortune or my left hand to help you. Lanyon, my life, my honour, my reason, are all at your mercy. If you fail me tonight, I am lost. You might suppose, after this **preface**, that I am going to ask you for something dishonourable to grant. Judge for yourself.

I want you to postpone all other engagements for tonight—ay, even if you were summoned to the bedside of an emperor, to take a cab, unless your carriage should be actually at the door, and, with this letter in your hand for consultation, to drive straight to my

DRAW *v.* **-ing, drew, drawn.**
 to pull, drag; to attract
  Synonyms: haul, tow, lug; lure, entice

MORBID (<u>mohr</u> bihd) *adj.*
 abnormally terrible and gloomy; relating to disease;
 gruesome
  Synonyms: dismal; pathological, unhealthy; grisly,
  macabre, unwholesome

house. Poole, my butler, has his orders; you will find him waiting your arrival with a locksmith. The door of my cabinet is then to be forced, and you are to go in alone, to open the glazed press (letter E) on the left hand, breaking the lock if it be shut, and to **draw** out, *with all its contents as they stand,* the fourth drawer from the top or (which is the same thing) the third from the bottom. In my extreme distress of mind, I have a **morbid** fear of misdirecting you, but even if I am in error, you may know the right drawer by its contents: some powders, a phial, and a paper book. This drawer I beg of you to carry back with you to Cavendish Square exactly as it stands.

That is the first part of the service. Now for the second. You should be back, if you set out at once on the receipt of this, long before midnight, but I will leave you that amount of margin, not only in the fear of one of those obstacles that can neither be prevented nor foreseen, but because an hour when your servants are in bed is to be preferred for what will then remain to do. At midnight, then, I have to ask you to be alone in your consulting-room, to admit with your own hand into the house a man who will present himself in my name, and to place in his hands the drawer that you will have brought with you from my cabinet. Then you will have played your part and earned my gratitude completely. Five minutes afterwards, if you insist upon an explanation, you will have understood that these arrangements are of capital importance, and that by the neglect of one of them, fantastic as they must appear, you might have charged your conscience with my death or the shipwreck of my reason.

TRIFLE (<u>trie</u> fuhl) *v.* **-ing,-ed.**
to waste time or money; to toy around with
Synonyms: squander; putter, fidget

Confident as I am that you will not **trifle** with this appeal, my heart sinks and my hand trembles at the bare thought of such a possibility. Think of me at this hour, in a strange place, labouring under a blackness of distress that no fancy can exaggerate, and yet well aware that, if you will but punctually serve me, my troubles will roll away like a story that is told. Serve me, my dear Lanyon, and save

Your friend,
H.J.

P.S.—I had already sealed this up when a fresh terror struck upon my soul. It is possible that the post office may fail me, and this letter not come into your hands until tomorrow morning. In that case, dear Lanyon, do my errand when it shall be most convenient for you in the course of the day, and once more expect my messenger at midnight. It may then already be too late, and if that night passes without event, you will know that you have seen the last of Henry Jekyll.

Upon the reading of this letter, I made sure my colleague was insane, but till that was proved beyond the possibility of doubt, I felt bound to do as he requested. The less I understood of this <u>farrago</u>, the less I was in a position to judge of its importance; and an appeal so worded could not be set aside without a grave responsibility. I rose accordingly from the table, got into a <u>hansom</u>, and drove straight to Jekyll's house. The butler was awaiting my arrival. He had received by the same post as mine a registered letter of instruction, and had sent at once for a locksmith and a carpenter. The tradesmen came while we were yet speaking, and we moved in a body to old Dr. Denman's surgical theatre, from which

PUNGENT (<u>puhn</u> juhnt) *adj.*
    strong or sharp in smell or taste
        Synonyms: acrid, penetrating, biting, caustic,
        piquant

VOLATILE (<u>vahl</u> iht uhl) (<u>vahl</u> ih tiel) *adj.*
    able to evaporate easily at normal temperatures;
    varying, inconstant
        Synonyms: vaporizable; changeable, fickle

WHET (weht) *v.* **-ting,-ted.**
    to sharpen, stimulate
        Synonyms: hone, edge, strop

(as you are doubtless aware) Jekyll's private cabinet is most conveniently entered. The door was very strong, the lock excellent. The carpenter avowed he would have great trouble, and have to do much damage, if force were to be used, and the locksmith was near despair. But this last was a handy fellow, and after two hours' work, the door stood open. The press marked E was unlocked, and I took out the drawer, had it filled up with straw and tied in a sheet, and returned with it to Cavendish Square.

Here I proceeded to examine its contents. The powders were neatly enough made up, but not with the nicety of the dispensing chemist, so that it was plain they were of Jekyll's private manufacture, and when I opened one of the wrappers, I found what seemed to me a simple crystalline salt of a white colour. The phial, to which I next turned my attention, might have been about half-full of a blood-red liquor, which was highly **pungent** to the sense of smell, and seemed to me to contain phosphorus and some **volatile** ether. At the other ingredients I could make no guess. The book was an ordinary version book, and contained little but a series of dates. These covered a period of many years, but I observed that the entries ceased nearly a year ago and quite abruptly. Here and there a brief remark was appended to a date, usually no more than a single word: "double" occurring perhaps six times in a total of several hundred entries, and once, very early in the list and followed by several marks of exclamation, "total failure!!!"

All this, though it **whetted** my curiosity, told me little that was definite. Here were a phial of some tincture, a paper of some salt, and the record of a series of experiments that had led (like too many of Jekyll's investigations) to no end of practical usefulness. How could the presence of these articles in my house affect either the honour, the sanity, or the life of my flighty

SAT VOCABULARY

IMPEDIMENT (ihm <u>pehd</u> uh muhnt) *n.*
barrier, obstacle; speech disorder
Synonyms: obstruction, hindrance, hurdle; lisp

CONSTRAINED (kuhn <u>straynd</u>) *adj.*
forced, impelled, not voluntary
Synonyms: restricted, controlled, calculated

DEBILITY (dih <u>bih</u> lih tee) *n.*
a state of weakness or feebleness
Synonyms: faintness, infirmity, exhaustion

CONSTITUTION (kahn stih <u>too</u> shuhn) *n.*
the physical structure or health of something or
someone; the sum of components, composition
Synonyms: disposition, nature, stature; formation,
design, architecture, make-up

INCIPIENT (ihn <u>sihp</u> ee uhnt) *adj.*
beginning to exist or appear, in an initial stage
Synonyms: dawning, nascent, inchoate

RIGOR (<u>rihg</u> uhr) *n.*
1. rigidity of muscles in the body
Synonyms: stiffness, inflexibility
2. hardship
Synonyms: severity, harshness, strictness

IDIOSYNCRATIC (ih dee uh sihn <u>kraa</u> tihk) *adj.*
peculiar in temperament, eccentric
Synonyms: quirky, odd

ACUTENESS (uh <u>kyoot</u> nehs) *n.*
sharpness, severity
Synonym: intensity

colleague? If his messenger could go to one place, why could he not go to another? And even granting some **impediment**, why was this gentleman to be received by me in secret? The more I reflected, the more convinced I grew that I was dealing with a case of <u>cerebral</u> disease; and though I dismissed my servants to bed, I loaded an old revolver, that I might be found in some posture of self-defence.

Twelve o'clock had scarce rung out over London, ere the knocker sounded very gently on the door. I went myself at the summons and found a small man crouching against the pillars of the portico.

"Are you come from Dr. Jekyll?" I asked.

He told me "yes" by a **constrained** gesture, and when I had bidden him enter, he did not obey me without a searching backward glance into the darkness of the square. There was a policeman not far off, advancing with his bull's eye open; and at the sight, I thought my visitor started and made greater haste.

These particulars struck me, I confess, disagreeably, and as I followed him into the bright light of the consulting-room, I kept my hand ready on my weapon. Here, at last, I had a chance of clearly seeing him. I had never set eyes on him before, so much was certain. He was small, as I have said. I was struck besides with the shocking expression of his face, with his remarkable combination of great muscular activity and great apparent **debility** of **constitution**, and—last but not least—with the odd, subjective disturbance caused by his neighbourhood. This bore some resemblance to **incipient rigor** and was accompanied by a marked sinking of the pulse. At the time, I set it down to some **idiosyncratic**, personal distaste, and merely wondered at the **acuteness** of the symptoms, but I have since had reason to believe the cause to lie much deeper in the

SOBER (<u>soh</u> buhr) *adj.*
    plain, self-controlled; serious; not intoxicated
        Synonyms: subdued, sedate; grave; dry, not drunk

LUDICROUS (<u>loo</u> dih kruhs) *adj.*
    laughable, ridiculous
        Synonyms: hilarious, absurd, foolish, silly,
        preposterous

DISPARITY (dih <u>spaar</u> ih tee) *n.*
    contrast, dissimilarity
        Synonyms: discrepancy, contradiction, divergence,
        incongruity

SOMBER (<u>sahm</u> buhr) *adj.*
    melancholy, dismal, dark and gloomy
        Synonyms: serious, grave, mournful, lugubrious,
        funereal

nature of man, and to turn on some nobler hinge than the principle of hatred.

This person (who had thus, from the first moment of his entrance, struck in me what I can only describe as a disgustful curiosity) was dressed in a fashion that would have made an ordinary person laughable. His clothes, that is to say, although they were of rich and **sober** fabric, were enormously too large for him in every measurement—the trousers hanging on his legs and rolled up to keep them from the ground, the waist of the coat below his haunches, and the collar sprawling wide upon his shoulders. Strange to relate, this **ludicrous accoutrement** was far from moving me to laughter. Rather, as there was something abnormal and misbegotten in the very essence of the creature that now faced me—something seizing, surprising and revolting. This fresh **disparity** seemed but to fit in with and to reinforce it, so that to my interest in the man's nature and character there was added a curiosity as to his origin, his life, his fortune and status in the world.

These observations, though they have taken so great a space to be set down in, were yet the work of a few seconds. My visitor was, indeed, on fire with **somber** excitement.

"Have you got it?" he cried. "Have you got it?" And so lively was his impatience that he even laid his hand upon my arm and sought to shake me.

I put him back, conscious at his touch of a certain icy pang along my blood. "Come, sir," said I. "You forget that I have not yet the pleasure of your acquaintance. Be seated, if you please." And I showed him an example, and sat down myself in my customary seat and with as fair an imitation of my ordinary manner to a patient, as the lateness of the hour, the nature of my preoccupations, and the horror I had of my visitor would suffer me to muster.

CIVILLY (<u>sih</u> vuh lee) *adv.*
  politely; publicly
    Synonyms: courteously; communally

SUSPENSE (suh <u>spents</u>) *n.*
  a feeling of anxiety caused by a mysterious situation
    Synonyms: apprehension, anticipation, waiting

PETRIFIED (<u>peh</u> trih fied) *adj.*
  paralyzed or stunned with fear; converted to stone
    Synonyms: dazed, stupefied, numb; mineralized

EFFERVESCE (eh fuhr <u>vehs</u>) *v.* **-ing,-ed.**
  to bubble; to be lively, show high spirits
    Synonyms: foam, froth, fizz; excite

AUDIBLY (<u>aw</u> dih blee) *adv.*
  in a manner capable of being heard, aloud
    Synonyms: detectably, perceptibly, loudly, plainly

EBULLITION (eh buh <u>lih</u> shuhn) *n.*
  the act of boiling or bubbling; exhilaration
    Synonyms: foaming, fermentation; zest

"I beg your pardon, Dr. Lanyon," he replied, **civilly** enough. "What you say is very well founded, and my impatience has shown its heels to my politeness. I come here at the instance of your colleague, Dr. Henry Jekyll, on a piece of business of some moment, and I understood . . ."—he paused and put his hand to his throat, and I could see, in spite of his collected manner, that he was wrestling against the approaches of the hysteria— "I understood, a drawer . . ."

But here I took pity on my visitor's **suspense**, and some perhaps on my own growing curiosity.

"There it is, sir," said I, pointing to the drawer where it lay on the floor behind a table, and still covered with the sheet.

He sprang to it, and then paused and laid his hand upon his heart; I could hear his teeth grate with the convulsive action of his jaws, and his face was so ghastly to see that I grew alarmed both for his life and reason.

"Compose yourself," said I.

He turned a dreadful smile to me, and, as if with the decision of despair, plucked away the sheet. At sight of the contents, he uttered one loud sob of such immense relief that I sat **petrified**. And the next moment, in a voice that was already fairly well under control, "Have you a graduated glass?" he asked.

I rose from my place with something of an effort and gave him what he asked.

He thanked me with a smiling nod, measured out a few minims of the red tincture, and added one of the powders. The mixture, which was at first of a reddish hue, began, in proportion as the crystals melted, to brighten in colour, to **effervesce audibly**, and to throw off small fumes of vapour. Suddenly, and at the same moment, the **ebullition** ceased, and the compound changed to a dark purple, which faded again more slowly to a watery green. My visitor, who had watched

SAT VOCABULARY

METAMORPHOSIS (meh tuh <u>mohr</u> fuh sihs) *n.*
   a change or transformation in appearance
      Synonyms: conversion, alteration, transfiguration

KEEN *adj.*
   intellectually sharp, perceptive; having a sharp edge
      Synonyms: acute, quick, canny; pointed, razorlike

SCRUTINY (<u>skroot</u> nee) *n.*
   careful observation
      Synonyms: examination, study, surveillance

PRODIGY (<u>prah</u> dih jee) *n.*
   an extraordinary event that inspires wonder; an
   exceptionally talented person
      Synonyms: marvel, miracle; genius

ENIGMA (eh <u>nihg</u> muh) *n.*
   a puzzle; an inexplicable event
      Synonyms: brainteaser, riddle; mystery

INEXPLICABLE (ihn ehk <u>splih</u> kuh buhl) *adj.*
   difficult to explain, baffling, mystifying
      Synonyms: unexplainable, incomprehensible

TRANSCENDENTAL (traan sehn <u>dehn</u> tuhl) *adj.*
   supernatural; able to rise above or go beyond
      Synonyms: otherworldly; surpassing, exceeding

DERIDE (dih <u>ried</u>) *v.* **-ing,-ed.**
   to mock, ridicule, make fun of
      Synonyms: taunt, jeer, insult, tease

these **metamorphoses** with a **keen** eye, smiled, set down the glass upon the table, and then turned and looked upon me with an air of **scrutiny**.

"And now," said he, "to settle what remains. Will you be wise? Will you be guided? Will you suffer me to take this glass in my hand, and to go forth from your house without further <u>parley</u>? Or has the greed of curiosity too much command of you? Think before you answer, for it shall be done as you decide. As you decide, you shall be left as you were before, and neither richer nor wiser, unless the sense of service rendered to a man in mortal distress may be counted as a kind of riches of the soul. Or, if you shall so prefer to choose, a new province of knowledge and new avenues to fame and power shall be laid open to you, here, in this room, upon the instant, and your sight shall be blasted by a **prodigy** to stagger the unbelief of Satan."

"Sir," said I, affecting a coolness that I was far from truly possessing, "you speak **enigmas**, and you will perhaps not wonder that I hear you with no very strong impression of belief. But I have gone too far in the way of **inexplicable** services to pause before I see the end."

"It is well," replied my visitor. "Lanyon, you remember your vows. What follows is under the seal of our profession. And now, you who have so long been bound to the most narrow and material views, you who have denied the virtue of **transcendental** medicine, you who have **derided** your superiors—behold!"

He put the glass to his lips and drank at one gulp. A cry followed. He reeled, staggered, clutched at the table and held on, staring with injected eyes, gasping with open mouth; and as I looked, there came, I thought, a change—he seemed to swell—his face became suddenly black, and the features seemed to melt and alter—and the next moment I had sprung to my feet and leaped

PRODIGY (<u>prah</u> dih jee) *n.*
an extraordinary event that inspires wonder; an
exceptionally talented person
Synonyms: marvel, miracle; genius

INCREDULOUS (ihn <u>krehj</u> uh luhs) *adj.*
skeptical, doubtful
Synonyms: disbelieving, suspicious

TURPITUDE (<u>tuhr</u> pih tood) *n.*
inherent vileness, foulness, depravity
Synonyms: baseness, immorality, wickedness

PENITENCE (<u>peh</u> nih tehnts) *n.*
sorrow expressed for sins or offenses, repentance
Synonyms: remorse, contrition, apology

back against the wall, my arm raised to shield me from that **prodigy**, my mind submerged in terror.

"Oh God!" I screamed, and "Oh God!" again and again, for there before my eyes—pale and shaken, and half fainting, and groping before him with his hands, like a man restored from death—there stood Henry Jekyll!

What he told me in the next hour I cannot bring my mind to set on paper. I saw what I saw, I heard what I heard, and my soul sickened at it. And yet, now when that sight has faded from my eyes, I ask myself if I believe it, and I cannot answer. My life is shaken to its roots, sleep has left me, the deadliest terror sits by me at all hours of the day and night. I feel that my days are numbered, and that I must die, and yet I shall die **incredulous**. As for the moral **turpitude** that man unveiled to me, even with tears of **penitence**, I cannot, even in memory, dwell on it without a start of horror. I will say but one thing, Utterson, and that (if you can bring your mind to credit it) will be more than enough. The creature who crept into my house that night was, on Jekyll's own confession, known by the name of Hyde and hunted for in every corner of the land as the murderer of Carew.

HASTIE LANYON

ENDOW (ehn <u>dow</u>) *v.* **-ing,-ed.**
to provide with something naturally or freely; to furnish with an income or grant
Synonyms: empower, support; grant, donate, bestow

INCLINE (ihn <u>klien</u>) *v.* **-ing,-ed.** *(See page 76.)*

DISPOSITION (dihs puh <u>zih</u> shuhn) *n.* *(See page 40.)*

RECONCILE (<u>reh</u> kuhn siel) *v.* **-ing,-ed.**
1. to accept
Synonyms: resign, submit
2. to resolve a dispute
Synonyms: agree, accommodate, rectify, reunite

IMPERIOUS (ihm <u>pihr</u> ee uhs) *adj.*
arrogantly self-assured, domineering, overbearing
Synonyms: authoritarian, despotic

COUNTENANCE (<u>kown</u> tuh nuhns) *n.* *(See page 96.)*

PROFOUND (pruh <u>fownd</u>) (proh <u>fownd</u>) *adj.*
deep, infinite; intelligent; difficult to understand
Synonyms: bottomless, unending; smart; weighty

DUPLICITY (doo <u>plih</u> sih tee) *n.*
the quality of being double; deception, dishonesty
Synonyms: duality, two-facedness; infidelity, disloyalty

MORBID (<u>mohr</u> bihd) *adj.* *(See page 104.)*

ASPIRATION (aa spuhr <u>ay</u> shuhn) *n.*
a great hope or goal
Synonyms: intention, purpose, expectation

DEGRADATION (day greh <u>day</u> shuhn) *n.*
the act of losing moral or intellectual character; the act of falling in rank or status
Synonyms: abasement, disgrace, shame; demotion

INVETERATELY (ihn <u>veht</u> uhr iht lee) *adv.*
incessantly, persistantly
Synonyms: habitually, chronically, continuously

HYPOCRITE (<u>hih</u> puh kriht) *n.*
person claiming beliefs or virtues he or she doesn't really possess
Synonyms: fraud, liar, sham, fake, phony

RESTRAINT (rih <u>straynt</u>) *n.*
control, repression, restriction; a rule or limitation
Synonyms: confinement; barrier, order, rein

DR. JEKYLL AND MR. HYDE

HENRY JEKYLL'S FULL STATEMENT OF THE CASE

I was born in the year 18—— to a large fortune, **endowed** besides with excellent parts, **inclined** by nature to industry, fond of the respect of the wise and good among my fellow-men, and thus, as might have been supposed, with every guarantee of an honourable and distinguished future. And indeed, the worst of my faults was a certain impatient gaiety of **disposition**, such as has made the happiness of many, but such as I found it hard to **reconcile** with my **imperious** desire to carry my head high and wear a more than commonly grave **countenance** before the public. Hence it came about that I concealed my pleasures, and that when I reached years of reflection, and began to look round me and take stock of my progress and position in the world, I stood already committed to a **profound duplicity** of life.

Many a man would have even <u>blazoned</u> such irregularities as I was guilty of, but from the high views that I had set before me, I regarded and hid them with an almost **morbid** sense of shame. It was thus rather the exacting nature of my **aspirations** than any particular **degradation** in my faults that made me what I was and, with even a deeper trench than in the majority of men, severed in me those provinces of good and ill which divide and compound man's dual nature. In this case, I was driven to reflect deeply and **inveterately** on that hard law of life which lies at the root of religion, and is one of the most plentiful springs of distress. Though so **profound** a double-dealer, I was in no sense a **hypocrite**. Both sides of me were in dead earnest. I was no more myself when I laid aside **restraint** and plunged in shame than when I laboured, in the eye of day, at the further-

TRANSCENDENTAL (traan sehn <u>dehn</u> tuhl) *adj.*
  supernatural; able to rise above or go beyond
    Synonyms: otherworldly; surpassing, exceeding

DRAW *v.* **-ing, drew, drawn.**
  1. to move steadily
    Synonyms: proceed, continue, progress
  2. to pull, drag; to attract
    Synonyms: haul, tow, lug; lure, entice

MULTIFARIOUS (muhl tuh <u>faar</u> ee uhs) *adj.*
  diverse
    Synonyms: various, multitudinal, populous

INCONGRUOUS (ihn <u>kahng</u> groo uhs) *adj.*
  incompatible, disagreeing
    Synonyms: inconsistent, unsuitable, inharmonious

DENIZEN (<u>dehn</u> ih zehn) *n.*
  a native, one who is very familiar with a certain place
    Synonyms: resident, citizen, inhabitant

INFALLIBLY (ihn <u>faal</u> uh blee) *adv.*
  without error
    Synonyms: certainly, guaranteed

ASPIRATION (aa spuhr <u>ay</u> shuhn) *n.*
  a great hope or goal
    Synonyms: intention, purpose, expectation

REMORSE (rih <u>mohrs</u>) *n.*
  a gnawing distress arising from a sense of guilt
    Synonyms: anguish, ruefulness, shame, penitence

STEADFASTLY (<u>stehd</u> faast lee) *adv.*
  with persistence; without wavering, loyally
    Synonyms: relentlessly, faithfully, constantly,
    staunchly

PENITENCE (<u>peh</u> nih tehnts) *n.*
  sorrow expressed for sins or offenses, repentance
    Synonyms: remorse, contrition, apology

EXTRANEOUS (ihk <u>stray</u> nee uhs) *adj.*
  irrelevant, unrelated, unnecessary
    Synonyms: immaterial, impertinent, extrinsic,
    foreign, alien

ance of knowledge or the relief of sorrow and suffering. And it chanced that the direction of my scientific studies, which led wholly towards the mystic and the **transcendental**, reacted and shed a strong light on this consciousness of the perennial war among my members.

With every day, and from both sides of my intelligence, the moral and the intellectual, I thus **drew** steadily nearer to that truth by whose partial discovery I have been doomed to such a dreadful shipwreck: that man is not truly one, but truly two. I say two, because the state of my own knowledge does not pass beyond that point. Others will follow, others will outstrip me on the same lines, and I hazard the guess that man will be ultimately known for a mere <u>polity</u> of **multifarious**, **incongruous** and independent **denizens**. I, for my part, from the nature of my life, advanced **infallibly** in one direction and in one direction only. It was on the moral side, and in my own person, that I learned to recognise the thorough and primitive duality of man. I saw that, of the two natures that contended in the field of my consciousness, even if I could rightly be said to be either, it was only because I was radically both. And from an early date, even before the course of my scientific discoveries had begun to suggest the most naked possibility of such a miracle, I had learned to dwell with pleasure, as a beloved daydream, on the thought of the separation of these elements. If each, I told myself, could but be housed in separate identities, life would be relieved of all that was unbearable. The unjust might go his way, delivered from the **aspirations** and **remorse** of his more upright twin, and the just could walk **steadfastly** and securely on his upward path, doing the good things in which he found his pleasure and no longer exposed to disgrace and **penitence** by the hands of this **extraneous** evil. It was the curse of mankind that these **incongruous** <u>faggots</u> were thus bound together—

TRANSIENCE (<u>traan</u> see uhnts) *n.*
  the state of being temporary or short-lived
    Synonyms: brevity, impermanence, evanescence

COUNTENANCE (<u>kown</u> tuh nuhns) *n.*
  appearance, facial expression
    Synonyms: face, features, visage

SCRUPLE (<u>skroo</u> puhl) *n.*
  1. a very tiny amount
    Synonyms: morsel, iota, trace
  2. an ethical and moral belief that prevents action; a hesitation caused by moral conscience
    Synonyms: principle; restraint, qualm, misgiving

INOPPORTUNITY (ihn ah pohr <u>toon</u> ih tee) *n.*
  an inappropriate or unfavorable act
    Synonyms: inconvenience

SINGULAR (<u>sihn</u> gyuh luhr) *adj.*
  uncommon, peculiar
    Synonyms: unusual, odd, rare, unique, individual

PROFOUND (pruh <u>fownd</u>) (proh <u>fownd</u>) *adj.*
  intelligent; deep, infinite; difficult to understand
    Synonyms: smart; bottomless, unending; weighty

that in the agonised womb of consciousness these polar twins should be continuously struggling. How, then, were they <u>dissociated</u>?

I was so far in my reflections when, as I have said, a side light began to shine upon the subject from the laboratory table. I began to perceive more deeply than it has ever yet been stated, the trembling <u>immateriality</u>, the mistlike **transience**, of this seemingly so solid body in which we walk attired. Certain agents I found to have the power to shake and to pluck back that fleshly <u>vestment</u>, even as a wind might toss the curtains of a pavilion. For two good reasons, I will not enter deeply into this scientific branch of my confession. First, because I have been made to learn that the doom and burthen of our life is bound forever on man's shoulders, and when the attempt is made to cast it off, it but returns upon us with more unfamiliar and more awful pressure. Second, because, as my narrative will make, alas, too evident, my discoveries were incomplete. Enough, then, that I not only recognised my natural body for the mere aura and <u>effulgence</u> of certain of the powers that made up my spirit, but managed to compound a drug by which these powers should be dethroned from their supremacy, and a second form and **countenance** substituted, nonetheless natural to me because they were the expression, and bore the stamp, of lower elements in my soul.

I hesitated long before I put this theory to the test of practice. I knew well that I risked death, for any drug that so potently controlled and shook the very fortress of identity might by the least **scruple** of an overdose or at the least **inopportunity** in the moment of exhibition, utterly blot out that <u>immaterial</u> <u>tabernacle</u> which I looked to it to change. But the temptation of a discovery so **singular** and **profound** at last overcame the suggestions of alarm. I had long since prepared my

EBULLITION (eh buh <u>lih</u> shuhn) *n.*
the act of boiling or bubbling; exhilaration
Synonyms: foaming, fermentation; zest

NOVELTY (<u>nah</u> vuhl tee) *n.*
something fresh and original, newness
Synonyms: surprise, change, innovation

OBLIGATION (ah blih <u>gay</u> shuhn) *n.*
a requirement or force to obey; a sense of duty or promise
Synonyms: constraint, bind, commitment; responsibility

EXULT (ihg <u>suhlt</u>) *v.* **-ing,-ed.**
to be extremely joyful, to rejoice
Synonyms: celebrate, delight, jubilate

CONCEPTION (kuhn <u>sehp</u> shuhn) *n.*
1. a new start or beginning
Synonyms: entrance, origin
2. the creation of an idea
Synonyms: abstraction, invention, innovation

RIGOROUS (<u>rih</u> guhr uhs) *adj.*
intense, strict
Synonyms: rigid, uncompromising, severe

<u>tincture</u>. I purchased at once, from a firm of wholesale chemists, a large quantity of a particular salt, which I knew, from my experiments, to be the last ingredient required. And late one accursed night, I compounded the elements, watched them boil and smoke together in the glass, and when the **ebullition** had subsided, with a strong glow of courage, drank off the potion.

The most racking pangs succeeded: a grinding in the bones, deadly nausea, and a horror of the spirit that cannot be exceeded at the hour of birth or death. Then these agonies began swiftly to subside, and I came to myself as if out of a great sickness. There was something strange in my sensations, something indescribably new and, from its very **novelty**, incredibly sweet. I felt younger, lighter, happier in body. Within I was conscious of a heady recklessness, a current of disordered sensual images running like a mill race in my fancy, a solution of the bonds of **obligation**, an unknown but not an innocent freedom of the soul. I knew myself, at the first breath of this new life, to be more wicked, tenfold more wicked, sold a slave to my original evil. And the thought, in that moment, braced and delighted me like wine. I stretched out my hands, **exulting** in the freshness of these sensations, and in the act, I was suddenly aware that I had lost stature.

There was no mirror at that date in my room. That which stands beside me as I write was brought there later on, and for the very purpose of those transformations. The night, however, was far gone into the morning—the morning, black as it was, was nearly ripe for the **conception** of the day. The inmates of my house were locked in the most **rigorous** hours of slumber; and I determined, flushed as I was with hope and triumph, to venture in my new shape as far as to my bedroom. I crossed the yard, wherein the constellations looked down upon me, I could have thought, with wonder, the

SAT VOCABULARY

VIGILANCE (<u>vih</u> juh lehnts) *n.*
attention, watchfulness
Synonyms: alertness, awareness, care

DISCLOSE (dihs <u>klohs</u>) *v.* **-ing,-ed.**
to expose, divulge
Synonyms: confess, reveal, impart

EFFICACY (<u>eff</u> uh kuh se) *n.*
effectiveness, efficiency
Synonym: potency

ROBUST (roh <u>buhst</u>) *adj.*
strong and healthy, hardy
Synonyms: vigorous, sturdy

DEPOSE (dih <u>pohs</u>) *v.* **-ing,-ed.**
to remove from a high position; to testify
Synonyms: dethrone, overthrow, displace; declare, charge, affirm

COUNTENANCE (<u>kown</u> tuh nuhns) *n.*
appearance, facial expression
Synonyms: face, features, visage

DEFORMITY (dih <u>fohr</u> mih tee) *n.*
disfigurement
Synonyms: malformation, disproportion

REPUGNANCE (rih <u>puhg</u> nehnts) *n.*
strong dislike, distaste, or antagonism; an instance of contradiction or inconsistency
Synonyms: repulsion, hatred, aversion

MISGIVING (mihs <u>gihv</u> ihng) *n.*
a feeling of apprehension, doubt, sense of foreboding
Synonyms: distrust, presentiment, qualm, disquiet

first creature of that sort that their unsleeping **vigilance** had yet **disclosed** to them. I stole through the corridors, a stranger in my own house, and coming to my room, I saw for the first time the appearance of Edward Hyde.

I must here speak by theory alone, saying not that which I know, but that which I suppose to be most probable. The evil side of my nature, to which I had now transferred the stamping **efficacy**, was less **robust** and less developed than the good which I had just **deposed**. Again, in the course of my life, which had been, after all, nine-tenths a life of effort, virtue and control, it had been much less exercised and much less exhausted. And hence, as I think, it came about that Edward Hyde was so much smaller, slighter, and younger than Henry Jekyll. Even as good shone upon the **countenance** of the one, evil was written broadly and plainly on the face of the other. Evil besides (which I must still believe to be the lethal side of man) had left on that body an imprint of **deformity** and decay. And yet when I looked upon that ugly idol in the glass, I was conscious of no **repugnance**, rather of a leap of welcome. This, too, was myself. It seemed natural and human. In my eyes it bore a livelier image of the spirit, it seemed more express and single, than the imperfect and divided **countenance** I had been hitherto accustomed to call mine. And insofar I was doubtless right. I have observed that when I wore the semblance of Edward Hyde, none could come near to me at first without a visible **misgiving** of the flesh. This, as I take it, was because all human beings, as we meet them, are <u>commingled</u> out of good and evil, and Edward Hyde, alone in the ranks of mankind, was pure evil.

I lingered but a moment at the mirror. The second and conclusive experiment had yet to be attempted. It yet remained to be seen if I had lost my identity beyond redemption and must flee before daylight from a house

PIOUS (<u>pie</u> uhs) *adj.*
dedicated, devout, extremely religious
Synonyms: observant, reverent, sanctimonious

ASPIRATION (aa spuhr <u>ay</u> shuhn) *n.*
a great hope or goal
Synonyms: intention, purpose, expectation

DIABOLICAL (die uh <u>bah</u> lih kuhl) *adj.*
characteristic of the devil
Synonyms: fiendish, wicked, evil

DISPOSITION (dihs puh <u>zih</u> shuhn) *n.*
mood or temperament
Synonyms: behavior, tendency, inclination, nature

INCONGRUOUS (ihn <u>kahng</u> groo uhs) *adj.*
incompatible, disagreeing
Synonyms: inconsistent, unsuitable, inharmonious

AVERSION (uh <u>vuhr</u> zhuhn) *n.*
intense dislike
Synonyms: antagonism, antipathy, abhorrence,
repulsion, repugnance

DISPOSE (dih <u>spohz</u>) *v.* **-ing,-ed.**
1. to incline or give a tendency to; to put in place,
to settle
Synonyms: determine, motivate; organize, position
2. to get rid of
Synonyms: discard, throw out

INCOHERENCY (ihn koh <u>hihr</u> uhnt see) *n.*
lack of cohesion or connection; the inability to
express one's thoughts in a clear or orderly manner
Synonyms: disorder, disarray; confusion

that was no longer mine, and hurrying back to my cabinet, I once more prepared and drank the cup, once more suffered the pangs of dissolution, and came to myself once more with the character, the stature, and the face of Henry Jekyll.

That night I had come to the fatal crossroads. Had I approached my discovery in a more noble spirit, had I risked the experiment while under the empire of generous or **pious aspirations**, all must have been otherwise, and from these agonies of death and birth I had come forth an angel instead of a fiend. The drug had no discriminating action. It was neither **diabolical** nor divine. It but shook the doors of the prisonhouse of my **disposition**, and, like the captives of Philippi, that which stood within ran forth. At that time my virtue slumbered. My evil, kept awake by ambition, was alert and swift to seize the occasion, and the thing that was projected was Edward Hyde. Hence, although I had now two characters as well as two appearances, one was wholly evil and the other was still the old Henry Jekyll, that **incongruous** compound of whose reformation and improvement I had already learned to despair. The movement was thus wholly toward the worse.

Even at that time, I had not yet conquered my **aversion** to the dryness of a life of study. I would still be merrily **disposed** at times, and as my pleasures were (to say the least) undignified, and I was not only well known and highly considered, but growing towards the elderly man, this **incoherency** of my life was daily growing more unwelcome. It was on this side that my new power tempted me until I fell in slavery. I had but to drink the cup, to doff at once the body of the noted professor, and to assume, like a thick cloak, that of Edward Hyde. I smiled at the notion. It seemed to me at the time to be humorous, and I made my preparations with the most studious care. I took and furnished that house in

UNSCRUPULOUS (uhn <u>skroop</u> yuh luhs) *adj.*
immoral, dishonest; hasty and imprecise
Synonyms: unrestrained, deceitful; unconscientious

PARRY (<u>paa</u> ree) *v.* **-ing,-ied.**
to ward off or evade, especially by a quick-witted answer
Synonyms: avoid, repel

PECUNIARY (pih <u>kyoo</u> nee ayr ee) *adj.*
relating to money
Synonyms: monetary, economic, financial

FORTIFY (<u>fohr</u> tih fie) *v.* **-ing,-ed.**
to make strong, to reinforce or secure
Synonyms: invigorate, strengthen, energize, support

IMMUNITY (ih <u>myoo</u> nih tee) *n.*
exemption; protection from harm or disease
Synonyms: advantage, freedom, privelege; resistance

GENIAL (<u>jeen</u> yuhl) (<u>jee</u> nee uhl) *adj.*
pleasant and friendly; favorable to growth or comfort
Synonyms: nice, amiable; productive, generative

VICARIOUS (vie <u>kaar</u> ee uhs) *adj.*
substitute, surrogate; enjoyed through imagined participation in another's experience
Synonyms: proxy, delegated; second-hand

DEPRAVITY (dih <u>praav</u> ih tee) *n.*
sinfulness, moral corruption
Synonyms: decadence, debauchery, enormity, degradation

Soho to which Hyde was tracked by the police, and engaged as housekeeper a creature whom I well knew to be silent and **unscrupulous**. On the other side, I announced to my servants that a Mr. Hyde (whom I described) was to have full liberty and power about my house in the square, and to **parry** mishaps, I even called and made myself a familiar object in my second character. I next drew up that will to which you so much objected, so that if anything befell me in the person of Dr. Jekyll, I could enter on that of Edward Hyde without **pecuniary** loss. And thus **fortified**, as I supposed, on every side, I began to profit by the strange **immunities** of my position.

Men have before hired bravos to transact their crimes, while their own person and reputation sat under shelter. I was the first that ever did so for his pleasures. I was the first that could thus plod in the public eye with a load of **genial** respectability and in a moment, like a schoolboy, strip off these lendings and spring headlong into the sea of liberty. But for me, in my impenetrable mantle, the safety was complete. Think of it—I did not even exist! Let me but escape into my laboratory door, give me but a second or two to mix and swallow the draught that I had always standing ready, and whatever he had done, Edward Hyde would pass away like the stain of breath upon a mirror. And there in his stead, quietly at home, trimming the midnight lamp in his study, a man who could afford to laugh at suspicion, would be Henry Jekyll.

The pleasures which I made haste to seek in my disguise were, as I have said, undignified; I would scarce use a harder term. But in the hands of Edward Hyde they soon began to turn towards the monstrous. When I would come back from these excursions, I was often plunged into a kind of wonder at my **vicarious depravity**. This familiar that I called out of my own soul

MALIGN (muh <u>lien</u>) *adj.*
 evil in influence or effect; aggressively malicious;
 tending to produce death
  Synonyms: vindictive, threatening; destructive,
  harmful; lethal, fatal

BESTIAL (<u>behs</u> chuhl) (<u>bees</u> chuhl) *adj.*
 beastly, animal-like
  Synonyms: brutish, inhuman, savage

AVIDITY (aa <u>vihd</u> ih tee) *n.*
 greedy desire; enthusiasm
  Synonyms: craving, ardor; interest

INSIDIOUSLY (ihn <u>sihd</u> ee uhs lee) *adv.*
 treacherously, deviously
  Synonyms: deceitfully, perfidiously, alluringly

UNIMPAIRED (uhn ihm <u>payrd</u>) *adj.*
 undamaged, not injured
  Synonyms: unharmed, unspoiled

INFAMY (<u>ihn</u> fuh mee) *n.*
 reputation for bad deeds
  Synonyms: disgrace, dishonor, shame, ignominy

CONNIVE (kuh <u>niev</u>) *v.* **-ing,-ed.**
 to conspire, scheme
  Synonyms: collude, plot, contrive

CHASTISEMENT (<u>chaa</u> stiez mehnt) *n.*
 punishment, discipline, scolding
  Synonyms: castigation, penalty

PACIFY (<u>paa</u> suh fie) *v.* **-ing,-ied.**
 to restore calm, bring peace
  Synonyms: mollify, conciliate, appease, placate

and sent forth alone to do his good pleasure was a being inherently **malign** and villainous. His every act and thought centered on self, drinking pleasure with **bestial avidity** from any degree of torture to another, relentless like a man of stone. Henry Jekyll stood at times aghast before the acts of Edward Hyde, but the situation was apart from ordinary laws, and **insidiously** relaxed the grasp of conscience. It was Hyde, after all, and Hyde alone, that was guilty. Jekyll was no worse; he woke again to his good qualities seemingly **unimpaired**. He would even make haste, where it was possible, to undo the evil done by Hyde. And thus his conscience slumbered.

Into the details of the **infamy** at which I thus **connived** (for even now I can scarce grant that I committed it) I have no design of entering. I mean but to point out the warnings and the successive steps with which my **chastisement** approached. I met with one accident which, as it brought on no consequence, I shall no more than mention. An act of cruelty to a child aroused against me the anger of a passerby, whom I recognised the other day in the person of your kinsman. The doctor and the child's family joined him. There were moments when I feared for my life, and at last, in order to **pacify** their too just resentment, Edward Hyde had to bring them to the door and pay them in a cheque drawn in the name of Henry Jekyll. But this danger was easily eliminated from the future by opening an account at another bank in the name of Edward Hyde himself. And when, by sloping my own hand backwards, I had supplied my double with a signature, I thought I sat beyond the reach of fate.

Some two months before the murder of Sir Danvers, I had been out for one of my adventures, had returned at a late hour, and woke the next day in bed with somewhat odd sensations. It was in vain I looked about me; in vain I saw the decent furniture and tall proportions of my

COMELY (<u>kuhm</u> lee) *adj.*
physically graceful and beautiful
Synonyms: attractive, becoming, pretty

PALLOR (<u>paal</u> uhr) *n.*
extreme paleness of the skin
Synonyms: lividity, wanness

room in the square; in vain that I recognised the pattern of the bed curtains and the design of the mahogany frame. Something still kept insisting that I was not where I was, that I had not wakened where I seemed to be, but in the little room in Soho where I was accustomed to sleep in the body of Edward Hyde. I smiled to myself and in my psychological way, began lazily to inquire into the elements of this illusion, occasionally, even as I did so, dropping back into a comfortable morning doze. I was still so engaged when, in one of my more wakeful moments, my eye fell upon my hand. Now, the hand of Henry Jekyll (as you have often remarked) was professional in shape and size; it was large, firm, white and **comely**. But the hand which I now saw, clearly enough in the yellow light of a mid-London morning, lying half shut on the bedclothes, was lean, <u>corded</u>, knuckly, of a dusky **pallor**, and thickly shaded with a <u>swart</u> growth of hair. It was the hand of Edward Hyde.

I must have stared upon it for nearly half a minute, sunk as I was in the mere stupidity of wonder, before terror woke up in my breast as sudden and startling as the crash of cymbals, and bounding from my bed, I rushed to the mirror. At the sight that met my eyes, my blood was changed into something exquisitely thin and icy. Yes, I had gone to bed Henry Jekyll, I had awakened Edward Hyde. How was this to be explained? I asked myself, and then, with another bound of terror—how was it to be remedied? It was well on in the morning, the servants were up, all my drugs were in the cabinet—a long journey down two pairs of stairs, through the back passage, across the open court, and through the anatomical theatre, from where I was then standing horror-struck. It might indeed be possible to cover my face, but of what use was that, when I was unable to conceal the alteration in my stature? And then, with an over-powering sweetness of relief, it came back upon my

DRAW *v.* **-ing, drew, drawn.**
  to pull away, drag; to attract
    Synonyms: haul, tow, lug; lure, entice

INEXPLICABLE (ihn ehk <u>splih</u> kuh buhl) *adj.*
  difficult to explain, baffling, mystifying
    Synonyms: unexplainable, incomprehensible

IRREVOCABLY (ih rehv <u>oh</u> kuh blee) *adv.*
  conclusively, irreversibly
    Synonyms: permanently, indelibly, irreparably

OBLIGE (uh <u>bliej</u>) *v.* **-ing,-ed.**
  to require or force someone to obey
    Synonyms: compel, constrain, bind, favor

mind that the servants were already used to the coming and going of my second self. I had soon dressed, as well as I was able, in clothes of my own size, had soon passed through the house, where Bradshaw stared and **drew** back at seeing Mr. Hyde at such an hour and in such a strange array, and ten minutes later, Dr. Jekyll had returned to his own shape and was sitting down, with a darkened brow, to make a <u>feint</u> of breakfasting.

Small indeed was my appetite. This **inexplicable** incident, this reversal of my previous experience, seemed, like the Babylonian finger on the wall, to be spelling out the letters of my judgment, and I began to reflect more seriously than ever before on the issues and possibilities of my double existence. That part of me which I had the power of projecting had lately been much exercised and nourished. It had seemed to me of late as though the body of Edward Hyde had grown in stature, as though (when I wore that form) I were conscious of a more generous tide of blood, and I began to spy a danger that, if this were much prolonged, the balance of my nature might be permanently overthrown, the power of voluntary change be forfeited, and the character of Edward Hyde become **irrevocably** mine. The power of the drug had not been always equally displayed. Once, very early in my career, it had totally failed me. Since then I had been **obliged** on more than one occasion to double, and once, with infinite risk of death, to <u>treble</u> the amount, and these rare uncertainties had cast hitherto the sole shadow on my contentment. Now, however, and in the light of that morning's accident, I was led to <u>remark</u> that whereas, in the beginning, the difficulty had been to throw off the body of Jekyll, it had of late gradually but decidedly transferred itself to the other side. All things therefore seemed to point to this: that I was slowly losing hold of my original and better self, and becoming slowly incorporated with my second and worse.

SAT VOCABULARY

FACULTY (<u>faa</u> kuhl tee) *n.*
the ability to act or do
Synonyms: aptitude, capability, sense, skill

APPREHENSION (aa prih <u>hehn</u> shuhn) *n.*
suspicion or fear of future or unknown evil; the act
of perceiving or comprehending; a legal seizure
Synonyms: concern, worry; understanding; capture

INDIFFERENT (ihn <u>dihf</u> ruhnt) (ihn <u>dihf</u> uhr uhnt) *adj.*
uncaring, unbiased
Synonyms: unconcerned, detached, uninterested,
apathetic

INDIFFERENCE (ihn <u>dihf</u> ruhnts) *n.*
lack of caring
Synonyms: detachment, disinterest, apathy

INDULGE (ihn <u>duhlj</u>) *v.* **-ing,-ed.**
to give in to a craving or desire
Synonyms: humor, gratify, allow, pamper

ASPIRATION (aa spuhr <u>ay</u> shuhn) *n.*
a great hope or goal
Synonyms: intention, purpose, expectation

ABSTINENCE (<u>aab</u> stih nihnts) *n.*
the act of refraining from some activity or action
Synonyms: temperance, self-restraint

INDUCEMENT (ih <u>doos</u> mehnt) *n.*
something that persuades, an incentive
Synonyms: motive, urging, encouragement

RESOLUTE (reh suh <u>loot</u>) *adj.*
determined; with a clear purpose
Synonyms: firm, unwavering; intent, resolved

Between these two I now felt I had to choose. My two natures had memory in common, but all other **faculties** were most unequally shared between them. Jekyll (who was a <u>composite</u>) now with the most sensitive **apprehensions**, now with a greedy gusto, projected and shared in the pleasures and adventures of Hyde. But Hyde was **indifferent** to Jekyll, or but remembered him as the mountain bandit remembers the cavern in which he conceals himself from pursuit. Jekyll had more than a father's interest; Hyde had more than a son's **indifference**. To cast in my lot with Jekyll was to die to those appetites which I had long secretly **indulged** and had of late begun to pamper. To cast it in with Hyde was to die to a thousand interests and **aspirations**, and to become, at a blow and forever, despised and friendless. The bargain might appear unequal, but there was still another consideration in the scales. For while Jekyll would suffer smartingly in the fires of **abstinence**, Hyde would be not even conscious of all that he had lost. Strange as my circumstances were, the terms of this debate are as old and commonplace as man. Much the same **inducements** and alarms cast the die for any tempted and trembling sinner, and it fell out with me, as it falls with so vast a majority of my fellows, that I chose the better part and was found wanting in the strength to keep to it.

Yes, I preferred the elderly and discontented doctor, surrounded by friends and cherishing honest hopes, and bade a **resolute** farewell to the liberty, the comparative youth, the light step, leaping pulses and secret pleasures that I had enjoyed in the disguise of Hyde. I made this choice perhaps with some unconscious reservation, for I neither gave up the house in Soho, nor destroyed the clothes of Edward Hyde, which still lay ready in my cabinet. For two months, however, I was true to my determination; for two months I led a life of such

INSENSATE (ihn <u>sehn</u> sayt) (ihn <u>sehn</u> siht) *adj.*
without sense or human feeling; lacking sensation, unconscious
> Synonyms: cold-blooded; inanimate, numb

PROPENSITY (pruh <u>pehn</u> suh tee) *n.*
inclination, tendency
> Synonyms: predilection, bias, leaning, penchant, proclivity

TEMPEST (<u>tehm</u> pehst) *n.*
rage or fury; a storm
> Synonyms: tumult, turbulence, torrent; inclemency

CIVILITY (sih <u>vihl</u> ih tee) *n.*
a courteous behavior or politeness
> Synonyms: compliment, pleasantry

PROVOCATION (proh vah <u>kay</u> shuhn) *n.*
something that provokes a response, such as anger or disagreement
> Synonyms: controversy, stimulation, contention

DISPERSE (dihs <u>puhrs</u>) *v.* **-ing,-ed.**
to scatter, to break up
> Synonyms: dissipate, disintegrate, dispel

severity as I had never before attained to, and enjoyed the compensations of an approving conscience. But time began at last to obliterate the freshness of my alarm. The praises of conscience began to grow into a thing of course; I began to be tortured with throes and longings, as of Hyde struggling after freedom; and at last, in an hour of moral weakness, I once again compounded and swallowed the transforming <u>draught</u>.

I do not suppose that when a drunkard reasons with himself upon his vice, he is once out of five hundred times affected by the dangers that he runs through his <u>brutish</u> physical insensibility. Neither had I, long as I had considered my position, made enough allowance for the complete moral insensibility and **insensate** readiness to evil which were the leading characters of Edward Hyde. Yet it was by these that I was punished. My devil had been long caged—he came out roaring. I was conscious, even when I took the <u>draught</u>, of a more unbridled, a more furious **propensity** to ill. It must have been this, I suppose, that stirred in my soul that **tempest** of impatience with which I listened to the **civilities** of my unhappy victim. I declare at least, before God, no man morally sane could have been guilty of that crime upon so pitiful a **provocation**, and that I struck in no more reasonable spirit than that in which a sick child may break a plaything. But I had voluntarily stripped myself of all those balancing instincts by which even the worst of us continues to walk with some degree of steadiness among temptations. And in my case, to be tempted, however slightly, was to fall.

Instantly the spirit of Hell awoke in me and raged. With a transport of glee, I mauled the unresisting body, tasting delight from every blow, and it was not till weariness had begun to succeed that I was suddenly, in the top fit of my delirium, struck through the heart by a cold thrill of terror. A mist **dispersed**. I saw my life to be

AVENGER (uh <u>vehn</u> juhr) *n.*
one who retaliates or takes revenge for an injury or crime
  Synonyms: punisher, vindicator

REMORSE (rih <u>mohrs</u>) *n.*
a gnawing distress arising from a sense of guilt
  Synonyms: anguish, ruefulness, shame, penitence

SELF-INDULGENCE (sehlf ihn <u>duhl</u> jehns) *n.*
lenience, the act of giving into one's desires
  Synonyms: self-gratification, tolerance, pampering

INIQUITY (ih <u>nihk</u> wih tee) *n.*
sin, evil act
  Synonyms: immorality, injustice, wickedness, vice

ACUTENESS (uh <u>kyoot</u> nehs) *n.*
sharpness, severity
  Synonym: intensity

HUMILITY (hyoo <u>mihl</u> ih tee) *n.*
humbleness
  Synonyms: modesty, reserve, lowliness, timidity

RENUNCIATION (rih nuhn see <u>ay</u> shuhn) *n.*
the act of declaring that something is disowned or no longer recognized or accepted
  Synonyms: rejection, abandonment

PATENT (<u>paa</u> tehnt) *adj.*
obvious, unconcealed
  Synonyms: apparent, clear, distinct, evident, manifest

forfeit and fled from the scene of these excesses, at once glorying and trembling, my lust of evil gratified and stimulated, my love of life screwed to the topmost peg. I ran to the house in Soho and (to make assurance doubly sure) destroyed my papers. Thence I set out through the lamplit streets, in the same divided ecstasy of mind, gloating on my crime, light-headedly devising others in the future, and yet still hastening and still harkening in my wake for the steps of the **avenger**. Hyde had a song upon his lips as he compounded the <u>draught</u>, and as he drank it pledged the dead man. The pangs of transformation had not done tearing him, before Henry Jekyll, with streaming tears of gratitude and **remorse**, had fallen upon his knees and lifted his clasped hand to God. The veil of **self-indulgence** was rent from head to foot; I saw my life as a whole. I followed it up from the days of childhood, when I had walked with my father's hand, and through the self-denying toils of my professional life, to arrive again and again, with the same sense of unreality, at the damned horrors of the evening. I could have screamed aloud, I sought with tears and prayers to smother down the crowd of hideous images and sounds with which my memory swarmed against me. And still, between the petitions, the ugly face of my **iniquity** stared into my soul. As the **acuteness** of this **remorse** began to die away, it was succeeded by a sense of joy. The problem of my conduct was solved. Hyde was henceforth impossible; whether I would or not, I was now confined to the better part of my existence, and, oh, how I rejoiced to think it! With what willing **humility** I embraced anew the restrictions of natural life! With what sincere **renunciation** I locked the door by which I had so often gone and come, and ground the key under my heel!

The next day came the news that the murder had been overlooked, that the guilt of Hyde was **patent** to

IMPULSE (<u>ihm</u> puhls) *n.*
  sudden tendency, inclination
    Synonyms: urge, whim

BUTTRESS (<u>buh</u> trihs) *v.* **-ing,-ed.**
  to reinforce or support
    Synonyms: bolster, brace, prop, strengthen

RESOLVE (rih <u>sahlv</u>) *v.* **-ing,-ed.**
  to determine or to make a firm decision about
    Synonyms: solve, decide

RESOLVE (rih <u>sahlv</u>) *n.*
  determination, a firm decision
    Synonyms: dedication, perseverance, willpower

BENEFICENT (buh <u>neh</u> fih sihnt) *adj.*
  characterized by kindness and goodness
    Synonyms: benevolent, gracious, philanthropic, kind

PENITENCE (<u>peh</u> nih tehnts) *n.*
  sorrow expressed for sins or offenses, repentance
    Synonyms: remorse, contrition, apology

INDULGE (ihn <u>duhlj</u>) *v.* **-ing,-ed.**
  to give in to a craving or desire
    Synonyms: humor, gratify, allow, pamper

RESUSCITATE (rih <u>suh</u> suh tayt) *v.* **-ing,-ed.**
  to revive, bring back to life
    Synonyms: restore, revivify, resurrect

TRIFLE (<u>trie</u> fuhl) *v.* **-ing,-ed.**
  to toy around with; to waste time or money
    Synonyms: putter, fidget; squander

CAPACIOUS (kuh <u>pay</u> shuhs) *adj.*
  extensive, large, roomy
    Synonyms: ample, commodious

CONDESCENSION (kahn dih <u>sehn</u> shuhn) *n.*
  an attitude of superiority
    Synonyms: patronization, smugness

SUBSEQUENT (<u>suhb</u> suh kwehnt) *adj.*
  following in time or order
    Synonyms: succeeding, next

the world, and that the victim was a man high in public estimation. It was not only a crime, it had been a tragic folly. I think I was glad to know it; I think I was glad to have my better **impulses** thus **buttressed** and guarded by the terrors of the scaffold. Jekyll was now my city of refuge, let but Hyde peep out an instant, and the hands of all men would be raised to take and slay him.

I **resolved** in my future conduct to redeem the past, and I can say with honesty that my **resolve** was fruitful of some good. You know yourself how earnestly in the last months of last year I laboured to relieve suffering. You know that much was done for others, and that the days passed quietly, almost happily for myself. Nor can I truly say that I wearied of this **beneficent** and innocent life; I think instead that I daily enjoyed it more completely, but I was still cursed with my duality of purpose, and as the first edge of my **penitence** wore off, the lower side of me, so long **indulged**, so recently chained down, began to growl for licence. Not that I dreamed of **resuscitating** Hyde; the bare idea of that would startle me to frenzy. No, it was in my own person that I was once more tempted to **trifle** with my conscience, and it was as an ordinary secret sinner that I at last fell before the assaults of temptation.

There comes an end to all things. The most **capacious** measure is filled at last, and this brief **condescension** to my evil finally destroyed the balance of my soul. And yet I was not alarmed; the fall seemed natural, like a return to the old days before I had made my discovery. It was a fine, clear January day, wet under foot where the frost had melted, but cloudless overhead, and the Regent's Park was full of winter <u>chirrupings</u> and sweet with spring odours. I sat in the sun on a bench, the animal within me licking the chops of memory, the spiritual side a little drowsed, promising **subsequent penitence**, but not yet moved to begin. After all, I

SAT VOCABULARY

QUALM (kwahlm) *n.*
a sudden feeling of sickness; a sudden feeling of doubt
Synonyms: queasiness; worry, scruple, misgiving

CONTEMPT (kuhn tehmpt) *n.*
disrespect, scorn
Synonyms: derision, disdain

OBLIGATION (ah blih gay shuhn) *n.*
a sense of duty or promise; a requirement or force to obey
Synonyms: responsibility; constraint, bind, committment

FACULTY (faa kuhl tee) *n.*
the ability to act or do
Synonyms: aptitude, capability, sense, skill

SUCCUMB (suh kuhm) *v.* **-ing,-ed.**
to give in to a force or desire; to die
Synonyms: yield, submit, surrender; collapse, expire

PREVAIL (prih vayl) *v.* **-ing,-ed.**
1. to persuade successfully
   Synonyms: induce, influence, prompt, convince
2. to succeed lastingly; to overcome
   Synonyms: persist, endure; dominate, triumph

reflected, I was like my neighbours. And then I smiled, comparing myself with other men, comparing my active goodwill with the lazy cruelty of their neglect. And at the very moment of that <u>vainglorious</u> thought, a **qualm** came over me, a horrid nausea and the most deadly shuddering. These passed away and left me faint, and then as in its turn the faintness subsided, I began to be aware of a change in the temper of my thoughts, a greater boldness, a **contempt** of danger, a solution of the bonds of **obligation**. I looked down; my clothes hung formlessly on my shrunken limbs, the hand that lay on my knee was <u>corded</u> and hairy. I was once more Edward Hyde. A moment before I had been safe of all men's respect, wealthy, beloved—the cloth laying for me in the dining-room at home. And now I was the common <u>quarry</u> of mankind, hunted, houseless, a known murderer, <u>thrall</u> to the <u>gallows</u>.

My reason wavered, but it did not fail me utterly. I have more than once observed that, in my second character, my **faculties** seemed sharpened to a point and my spirits more tensely elastic. Thus it came about that, where Jekyll perhaps might have **succumbed**, Hyde rose to the importance of the moment. My drugs were in one of the presses of my cabinet—how was I to reach them? That was the problem that (crushing my temples in my hands) I set myself to solve. The laboratory door I had closed. If I sought to enter by the house, my own servants would consign me to the <u>gallows</u>. I saw I must employ another hand, and thought of Lanyon. How was he to be reached? How persuaded? Supposing that I escaped capture in the streets, how was I to make my way into his presence? And how should I, an unknown and displeasing visitor, **prevail** on the famous physician to rifle the study of his colleague, Dr. Jekyll? Then I remembered that of my original character, one part remained to me: I could write my own hand. And once I

SAT VOCABULARY

KINDLING (<u>kihn</u> dlihng) *adj.*
  causing excitement or inspiration; igniting
    Synonyms: arousing, awakening; lighting, sparking

MIRTH (muhrth) *n.*
  laughter, frivolity, gaiety
    Synonyms: merriment, jollity, hilarity, glee

COUNTENANCE (<u>kown</u> tuh nuhns) *n.*
  appearance, facial expression
    Synonyms: face, features, visage

OBSEQUIOUSLY (uhb <u>see</u> kwee uhs lee) *adv.*
  overly submissively or attentively
    Synonyms: subordinately, menially, compliantly

ASTUTE (uh <u>stoot</u>) *adj.*
  smartly aware, cleverly intelligent
    Synonyms: insightful, perspicacious, shrewd,
    perceptive

NOCTURNAL (nok <u>tuhr</u> nuhl) *adj.*
  pertaining to night, active at night
    Synonyms: nightly, dark

had conceived that **kindling** spark, the way that I must follow became lighted up from end to end.

Thereupon, I arranged my clothes as best I could, and summoning a passing <u>hansom</u>, drove to an hotel in Portland Street, the name of which I chanced to remember. At my appearance (which was indeed comical enough, however tragic a fate these garments covered) the driver could not conceal his **mirth**. I gnashed my teeth upon him with a gust of devilish fury; and the smile withered from his face—happily for him—yet more happily for myself, for in another instant I had certainly dragged him from his perch. At the inn, as I entered, I looked about me with so black a **countenance** as made the attendants tremble. Not a look did they exchange in my presence; but **obsequiously** took my orders, led me to a private room, and brought me wherewithal to write. Hyde in danger of his life was a creature new to me: shaken with inordinate anger, strung to the pitch of murder, lusting to inflict pain. Yet the creature was **astute**; mastered his fury with a great effort of the will, composed his two important letters, one to Lanyon and one to Poole, and, that he might receive actual evidence of their being posted, sent them out with directions that they should be registered.

Thenceforward, he sat all day over the fire in the private room, gnawing his nails. There he dined, sitting alone with his fears, the waiter visibly <u>quailing</u> before his eye. And thence, when the night was fully come, he set forth in the corner of a closed cab, and was driven to and fro about the streets of the city. He, I say—I cannot say, I. That child of Hell had nothing human; nothing lived in him but fear and hatred. And when at last, thinking the driver had begun to grow suspicious, he discharged the cab and ventured on foot, attired in his misfitting clothes, an object marked out for observation, into the midst of the **nocturnal** passengers, these two

SAT VOCABULARY

BASE (bays) *adj.*
lacking qualities of higher mind or spirit
Synonyms: vulgar, corrupt, immoral, menial

TEMPEST (<u>tehm</u> pehst) *n.*
a storm; rage or fury
Synonyms: inclemency; tumult, turbulence, torrent

SKULK (skuhlk) *v.* **-ing,-ed.**
to move in a stealthy or cautious manner, to sneak
Synonyms: lurk, shirk, hide, evade, prowl

ABHORRENCE (uhb <u>hohr</u> ehnts) *n.*
loathing, detestation
Synonyms: hatred, condemnation, abomination, execration

PROSTRATION (prah <u>stray</u> shuhn) *n.*
exhaustion, weariness; collapse
Synonyms: tiredness; breakdown, downfall

STRINGENT (<u>strihn</u> juhnt) *adj.*
imposing severe, rigorous standards
Synonyms: restricted, tight, demanding

PROFOUND (pruh <u>fownd</u>) (proh <u>fownd</u>) *adj.*
deep, infinite; intelligent; difficult to understand
Synonyms: bottomless, unending; smart; thorough

AVAIL (uh <u>vayl</u>) *v.* **-ing,-ed.**
to be of use or advantage to; to make use of;
to result in
Synonyms: help, serve, benefit; employ; transpire, eventuate

APPALLING (uh <u>pahl</u> lihng) *adj.*
shocking, dismaying
Synonyms: horrifying, dreadful, ghastly, awful

base passions raged within him like a **tempest**. He walked fast, hunted by his fears, chattering to himself, **skulking** through the less frequented thoroughfares, counting the minutes that still divided him from midnight. Once a woman spoke to him, offering, I think, a box of lights. He <u>smote</u> her in the face, and she fled.

When I came to myself at Lanyon's, the horror of my old friend perhaps affected me somewhat. I do not know; it was at least but a drop in the sea to the **abhorrence** with which I looked back upon these hours. A change had come over me. It was no longer the fear of the <u>gallows</u>, it was the horror of being Hyde that racked me. I received Lanyon's <u>condemnation</u> partly in a dream. It was partly in a dream that I came home to my own house and got into bed. I slept after the **prostration** of the day with a **stringent** and **profound** slumber which not even the nightmares that wrung me could **avail** to break. I awoke in the morning shaken, weakened, but refreshed. I still hated and feared the thought of the brute that slept within me, and I had not of course forgotten the **appalling** dangers of the day before, but I was once more at home, in my own house and close to my drugs, and gratitude for my escape shone so strong in my soul that it almost rivalled the brightness of hope.

I was stepping leisurely across the court after breakfast, drinking the chill of the air with pleasure, when I was seized again with those indescribable sensations that heralded the change, and I had but the time to gain the shelter of my cabinet, before I was once again raging and freezing with the passions of Hyde. It took on this occasion a double dose to recall me to myself, and alas, six hours after, as I sat looking sadly in the fire, the pangs returned, and the drug had to be re-administered. In short, from that day forth it seemed only by a great effort as of gymnastics, and only under the immediate stimulation of the drug, that I was able to wear the

SAT VOCABULARY

COUNTENANCE (<u>kown</u> tuh nuhns) *n.*
appearance, facial expression
   Synonyms: face, features, visage

PREMONITORY (preh <u>mah</u> nih tohr ee) *adj.*
foreboding, ominous
   Synonyms: threatening, intuitive, prophetic

LANGUIDLY (<u>laang</u> gwihd lee) *adv.*
without energy, indifferently, slowly
   Synonyms: weakly, listlessly, sluggishly

DEFORMITY (dih <u>fohr</u> mih tee) *n.*
disfigurement
   Synonyms: malformation, disproportion

POIGNANT (<u>poy</u> nyaant) *adj.*
emotionally moving
   Synonyms: stirring, touching, piquant

AMORPHOUS (uh <u>mohr</u> fuhs) *adj.*
having no definite form
   Synonyms: shapeless, indistinct

GESTICULATE (jeh <u>stih</u> kyuh layt) *v.* **-ing,-ed.**
to make expressive gestures
   Synonyms: motion, indicate, signal, wave, flag

USURP (yoo <u>suhrp</u>) *v.* **-ing,-ed.**
to occupy instead, to assume a position; to seize by force
   Synonyms: preempt, displace; arrogate, appropriate

INSURGENT (ihn <u>suhr</u> juhnt) *adj.*
rebellious, insubordinate
   Synonyms: revolutionary, seditious

PREVAIL (prih <u>vayl</u>) *v.* **-ing,-ed.** *(See page 148.)*

DEPOSE (dih <u>pohs</u>) *v.* **-ing,-ed.**
to remove from a high position; to testify
   Synonyms: dethrone, overthrow, displace; declare, charge, affirm

countenance of Jekyll. At all hours of the day and night I would be taken with the **premonitory** shudder. Above all, if I slept, or even dozed for a moment in my chair, it was always as Hyde that I awakened. Under the strain of this continually impending doom and by the sleeplessness to which I now condemned myself, ay, even beyond what I had thought possible to man, I became, in my own person, a creature eaten up and emptied by fever, **languidly** weak both in body and mind, and solely occupied by one thought: the horror of my other self. But when I slept, or when the virtue of the medicine wore off, I would leap almost without transition (for the pangs of transformation grew daily less marked) into the possession of a fancy brimming with images of terror, a soul boiling with causeless hatreds, and a body that seemed not strong enough to contain the raging energies of life. The powers of Hyde seemed to have grown with the sickliness of Jekyll. And certainly the hate that now divided them was equal on each side. With Jekyll, it was a thing of vital instinct. He had now seen the full **deformity** of that creature that shared with him some of the phenomena of consciousness and was co-heir with him to death. And beyond these links of community, which in themselves made the most **poignant** part of his distress, he thought of Hyde, for all his energy of life, as of something not only hellish but inorganic. This was the shocking thing: that the slime of the pit seemed to utter cries and voices; that the **amorphous** dust **gesticulated** and sinned; that what was dead, and had no shape, should **usurp** the offices of life. And this again, that that **insurgent** horror was knit to him closer than a wife, closer than an eye, lay caged in his flesh, where he heard it mutter and felt it struggle to be born, and at every hour of weakness, and in the confidences of slumber, **prevailed** against him, and **deposed** him out of life. The hatred of Hyde for Jekyll was of a

SAT VOCABULARY

LOATHE (lohth) *v.* **-ing,-ed.**
to abhor, despise, hate
Synonyms: abominate, execrate, detest, condemn

DESPONDENCY (dih spahn duhn see) *n.*
discouragement and dejection
Synonyms: sadness, depression, desolation, forlornness

BLASPHEMY (blaas fuh mee) *n.*
an act of profanity, an act of reviling something sacred
Synonyms: curse, indignity, impiety, abuse, sacrilege

ABJECTION (aab jehk shuhn) *n.*
misery, unhappiness
Synonyms: despair, dreariness, despondency

ALLEVIATION (uh lee vee ay shuhn) *n.*
relief, partial improvement
Synonyms: comfort, salvation, help, aid

CALLOUSNESS (kaa luhs nehs) *n.*
insensitivity, rudeness, hardening
Synonyms: indifference, disinterest, heartlessness

ACQUIESCENCE (aak wee ehs ehnts) *n.*
acceptance; compliance
Synonyms: consent, concurrence; submission

CALAMITY (kuh laam ih tee) *n.*
misfortune; state of despair
Synonyms: disaster, cataclysm; misery

PROVISION (pruh vih zhuhn) *n.*
a stock of needed materials or supplies
Synonyms: equipment, necessities

EBULLITION (eh buh lih shuhn) *n.*
the act of boiling or bubbling; exhilaration
Synonyms: foaming, fermentation; zest

EFFICACY (eff uh kuh se) *n.*
effectiveness, efficiency
Synonym: potency

different order. His terror of the <u>gallows</u> drove him continually to commit temporary suicide and return to his subordinate station of a part instead of a person. But he **loathed** the necessity, he **loathed** the **despondency** into which Jekyll was now fallen, and he resented the dislike with which he was himself regarded. Hence the apelike tricks that he would play me, scrawling in my own hand **blasphemies** on the pages of my books, burning the letters and destroying the portrait of my father. And indeed, had it not been for his fear of death, he would long ago have ruined himself in order to involve me in the ruin. But his love of life is wonderful. I go further: I, who sicken and freeze at the mere thought of him, when I recall the **abjection** and passion of this attachment, and when I know how he fears my power to cut him off by suicide, I find it in my heart to pity him.

It is useless, and the time awfully fails me, to prolong this description. No one has ever suffered such torments, let that suffice. And yet even to these, habit brought—no, not **alleviation**—but a certain **callousness** of soul, a certain **acquiescence** of despair; and my punishment might have gone on for years, but for the last **calamity** which has now fallen, and which has finally severed me from my own face and nature. My **provision** of the salt, which had never been renewed since the date of the first experiment, began to run low. I sent out for a fresh supply, and mixed the <u>draught</u>. The **ebullition** followed, and the first change of colour, not the second. I drank it, and it was without efficiency. You will learn from Poole how I have had London ransacked; it was in vain, and I am now persuaded that my first supply was impure, and that it was that unknown impurity which lent **efficacy** to the <u>draught</u>.

About a week has passed, and I am now finishing this statement under the influence of the last of the old powders. This, then, is the last time, short of a miracle, that

PRUDENCE (<u>proo</u> dehnts) *n.*
carefulness, caution
   Synonyms: circumspection, deliberation,
   thoughtfulness

Henry Jekyll can think his own thoughts or see his own face (now how sadly altered!) in the glass. Nor must I delay too long to bring my writing to an end, for if my narrative has hitherto escaped destruction, it has been by a combination of great **prudence** and great good luck. Should the throes of change take me in the act of writing it, Hyde will tear it in pieces. But if some time shall have elapsed after I have laid it by, his wonderful selfishness and circumscription to the moment will probably save it once again from the action of his apelike spite. And indeed the doom that is closing on us both has already changed and crushed him. Half an hour from now, when I shall again and for ever <u>reindue</u> that hated personality, I know how I shall sit shuddering and weeping in my chair, or continue, with the most strained and fearstruck ecstasy of listening, to pace up and down this room (my last earthly refuge) and give ear to every sound of menace. Will Hyde die upon the scaffold? Or will he find the courage to release himself at the last moment? God knows; I am careless. This is my true hour of death, and what is to follow concerns another than myself. Here, then, as I lay down the pen, and proceed to seal up my confession, I bring the life of that unhappy Henry Jekyll to an end.

GLOSSARY

The following words appear <u>underlined</u> throughout the text:

à propos (<u>aap</u> ruh poh) *adj. French.*
   appropriate and pertinent to

accoutrement (uh <u>koo</u> truh mehnt) *n.*
   the clothing or apparel one is wearing

amity (<u>aam</u> ih tee) *n.*
   friendship, peaceful relation

apothecary (uh <u>pahth</u> ih kayr ee) *n.*
   an English doctor (outside England, it means *pharmacist*)

aptness (<u>aapt</u> nehs) *n.*
   suitableness, appropriateness

aught (aht) *pron.*
   all, anything

baize (bayz) *n.*
   durable fabric made of cotton or wool

blackguardly (<u>blaag</u> uhrd lee) *adj.*
   lowly and delinquent

blazon (<u>blay</u> zehn) *v.* **-ing,-ed.**
   to display or proclaim proudly, to publicize

brandish (<u>braan</u> dihsh) *v.* **-ing,-ed.**
   to wave or move in an aggressive manner

brutish (<u>broo</u> tihsh) *adj.*
   rough, crude, uncivilized, bestial

carbuncle (<u>kahr</u> bung kuhl) *n.*
   a deep-red precious stone

cerebral (suh <u>ree</u> bruhl) (<u>sehr</u> uh bruhl) *adj.*
   relating to the brain

cheval-glass (shuh <u>vaal</u> glaas) *n.*
   a full-length mirror mounted in a swivel frame

chirruping (<u>chuhr</u> uh pihng) *n.*
   a chirping or clicking sound, as made by birds

GLOSSARY

commingle (kuh <u>mihn</u> guhl) *v.* **-ing,-ed.**
to be mixed or combined together

composite (kuhm <u>pah</u> ziht) *n.*
something comprised of distinct parts or elements

condemnation (kahn dehm <u>nay</u> shuhn) *n.*
an expression of extreme disapproval

conveyancing (kuhn <u>vay</u> ehnt sihng) *n.*
the legal transferring of property titles between people

cord (kohrd) *n.*
a flexible and lengthy structure of the body, such as a tendon, nerve, or muscle

corded (<u>kohr</u> dihd) *adj.*
having or showing tendons, nerves, or muscles

cupola (<u>kyoo</u> puh luh) *n.*
a dome-like structure on a roof used to admit light

dissociate (dih <u>soh</u> shee ayt) (dih <u>soh</u> see ayt) *v.* **-ing,-ed.**
to separate, to disjoin

distained (dih <u>staynd</u>) *adj.*
discolored and tarnished

draught (drawft) (draaft) *n. British.*
1. a current of air in an enclosed space 2. a drink

eddy (<u>eh</u> dee) *n.*
a circular current of water, like a whirlpool

effulgence (if <u>fuhl</u> jehnts) *n.*
radiance, brillance, brightness

embattled (ehm <u>baa</u> tuhld) *adj.*
prepared for battle; in this case, wounded or assailed

emulously (<u>ehm</u> yuh luhs lee) *adv.*
amibitiously, with hopes of surpassing others

faggot (<u>faa</u> giht) *n.*
a bundle of sticks bound tightly together; in this case, a metaphor for the characters of Dr. Jekyll and Mr. Hyde

GLOSSARY

farrago (fuh <u>rah</u> goh) *n.*
a mixture or medley of very different things or ideas

feint (faynt) *n.*
a deceptive show, a distracting maneuver

fortnight (<u>fohrt</u> niet) *n.*
a two-week period of time

gallows (<u>gaa</u> lohs) *n.*
a structure with a suspended noose used for hanging

graduated (<u>graa</u> joo ay tihd) *adj.*
marked at various levels for measuring purposes

haggard (<u>haa</u> guhrd) *adj.*
appearing scrawny, well-worn, and faded

halloa (heh <u>loh</u>) *n.*
an interjection used to catch someone's attention

hansom (<u>haan</u> suhm) *n.*
a covered horse-drawn carriage

harpy (<u>hahr</u> pee) *n.*
an evil monster with a woman's head and vulture's
body; a fiercely malicious woman

heresy (<u>hehr</u> ih see) *n.* **heresies** *n.pl.*
a controversial opinion

holograph (<u>hahl</u> uh graaf) *n.*
a document handwritten entirely by the person who
signed it

immaterial (ih muh <u>teer</u> ee uhl) *adj.*
without form or body, incorporeal

immateriality (ih muh <u>teer</u> ee ahl ih tee) *n.*
lack of substance or body

imperial dye (ihm <u>peer</u> ee uhl die) *n.*
the dye, often purple, used to color and indicate royal
clothing

GLOSSARY

intercourse (<u>ihn</u> tuhr kohrs) *n.*
   communication between people

juggernaut (<u>juh</u> guhr nawt) *n.*
   an overwhelming, crushing force

ken (kehn) *n.*
   range of sight or understanding

lawny (<u>law</u> nee) *adj.*
   having a gauzy, linen-like texture

mangled (<u>maan</u> guhld) *adj.*
   mutilated, disfigured

mantle (<u>maan</u> tuhl) *n.*
   anything that covers or protects what is underneath it

minim (<u>mih</u> nihm) *n.*
   a very small unit of volume, similar to a drop

napery (<u>nay</u> puh ree) *n.*
   table linen

pall (pahl) *n.*
   a covering that obscures or gives a gloomy effect

parley (<u>pahr</u> lee) *n.*
   a discussion among enemies

pede claudo (<u>pay</u> deh <u>klaow</u> doh)
   a Latin proverb which means, "Retribution comes slowly, but surely."

peevishly (<u>pee</u> vihsh lee) *adv.*
   in a discontented and cranky manner

phial (fiel) (<u>fie</u> uhl) *n.*
   a small glass bottle, a vial

polity (<u>pahl</u> ih tee) *n.*
   a political or social organization

prohibition (proh ih <u>bihsh</u> uhn) *n.*
   a law or formal request that forbids or prohibits something

GLOSSARY

protégé (<u>proh</u> tih zhay) (proh tih <u>zhay</u>) *n.*
a person who is supported, trained, and/or protected by an influential person

quail (kwayl) *v.* **-ing,-ed.**
to back away in fear, to flinch, to cower

quarry (<u>kwah</u> ree) *n.*
prey, a hunted animal

reformation (reh fuhr <u>may</u> shuhn) *n.*
the act of changing for the better

reindue (ree ihn <u>doo</u>) (ree ihn <u>dyoo</u>) *v.* **-ing,-ed.**
to provide with moral qualities and traits

remark (rih <u>mahrk</u>) *v.* **-ing,-ed.**
to observe or notice

reputable (<u>rehp</u> yuh tuh buhl) *adj.*
honorable, praiseworthy

scanty (<u>skaan</u> tee) *adj.*
lacking sufficient details or words

slatternly (<u>slaa</u> tuhrn lee) *adj.*
slovenly and unkempt

smite (smiet) *v.* **-ing, smote.**
to strike with a heavy blow of the hand

superscribe (soo puhr <u>skrieb</u>) *v.* **-ing,-ed.**
to write on the outside of a letter or document

swart (swahrt) *adj.*
of a dark color

tabernacle (<u>taa</u> buhr naa kuhl) *n.*
a dwelling place

thrall (thrahl) *n.*
a servant or slave

tincture (<u>tihngk</u> shuhr) *n.*
a medicinal solution

GLOSSARY

treble (<u>treh</u> buhl) *v.* **-ing,-ed.**
to triple

troglodytic (troh gluh <u>dih</u> tihk) *adj.*
resembling a caveman

undemonstrative (uhn dih <u>mahn</u> struh tihv) *adj.*
unemotional, reserved

unimpressionable (uhn ihm <u>prehsh</u> ihn uh buhl) *adj.*
not easily influenced or impressed

unmanning (uhn <u>maan</u> ihng) *adj.*
able to strip one of his courage and virility

vainglorious (vayn <u>glohr</u> ee uhs) *adj.*
boastful, self-important

vestment (<u>vehst</u> mehnt) *n.*
a covering or garment, such as a robe

wrack (raak) *n.*
a thin, wispy cloud

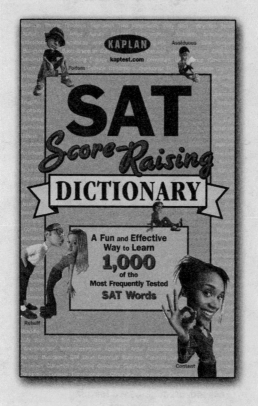

Introducing a smarter way to learn.

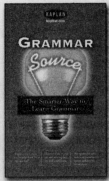

- Focused, practice-based learning
- Concepts for everyday life
- Recognition and recall exercises
- Quizzes throughout

Available wherever books are sold.